DECODING HELL'S PROPAGANDA

DECODING HELL'S PROPAGANDA

Sharpening Your Discernment

BRENDA KUNNEMAN

DESTINY IMAGE. PUBLISHERS, INC.

P.O. Box 310, Shippensburg, PA 17257-0310

"Speaking to the Purposes of God for This Generation and for the Generations to Come."

This book and all other Destiny Image, Revival Press, MercyPlace, Fresh Bread, Destiny Image Fiction, and Treasure House books are available at Christian bookstores and distributors worldwide.

For a U.S. bookstore nearest you, call 1-800-722-6774.

For more information on foreign distributors, call 717-532-3040.

Reach us on the Internet: www.destinyimage.com.

ISBN 13 Trade Paper: 978-0-7684-3229-9
ISBN 13 Hard Copy: 978-0-7684-3606-8
ISBN 13 Large Print: 978-0-7684-3607-5
ISBN 13 E-book: 978-0-7684-9080-0

For Worldwide Distribution, Printed in the U.S.A.

1 2 3 4 5 6 7 8 9 10 11 / 13 12 11 10

Dedication

I dedicate this book with deep appreciation to the remnant Church of believers who have given their lives, refused to compromise, and upheld the righteousness of the Gospel.

Acknowledgments

I express my thanks to my two wonderful sons, Matthew and Jonathan, for their patience and support while their mother was immersed in this project!

Endorsements

Most Christians have waged intellectual war against the New Age philosophies of our day. Unfortunately, I have watched many devoted Christians, even church leaders, fall prey to the systematic deception of satan. The answer to our dilemma is surprising. What the Church really needs is a strong dose of spiritual discernment followed by outright obedience. These issues are succinctly addressed by Brenda Kunneman in *Decoding Hell's Propaganda*. This book not only presents an explanation of how we are deceived but gives practical ways of escape.

This book is a must-read for emerging young leaders, established leaders, and the greater Christian community who want to make a difference for the Kingdom of God.

BISHOP HARRY R. JACKSON JR.
Senior Pastor of Hope Christian Church
Washington, DC
Founder and President
High Impact Leadership Coalition

Brenda's book could keep you out of a *ton of trouble*. We need to hear the voice of the Good Shepherd. Many times we are listening and following the voice of strangers. This book is a *must* for every Christian desiring wisdom in their daily walk.

DR. MARILYN HICKEY
President, Marilyn Hickey Ministries

Brenda Kunneman thoroughly understands and has identified the critical weaknesses of the "seeker-friendly" approach to the Gospel of our Lord and Savior Jesus Christ. Many of these same trends led to the rise of historic heresies in past centuries. The New Testament Gospels—when they are presented—are very clear regarding judgments and blessings. Brenda's book offers a clear warning to the Body of Christ.

REV. LOUIS P. SHELDON
Chairman and Founder, Traditional Values Coalition

The Church has lost its ability to separate the precious from the vile, and many churchgoers are about to experience the worst nightmare possible to man—hearing the Lord say, *"Depart from Me, I never knew you."* Self-help sermons and cheap grace are the norm today, often depicting "another Gospel" different from the one that will save men's souls. Brenda Kunneman powerfully exposes the work of satan, and this book is a must-read for anyone who desires to shine the light on satan's propaganda. I highly recommend it!

PASTOR LARRY GORDON
Senior Pastor, Cornerstone World Outreach
Sioux City, Iowa

Contents

Introduction

Propaganda (prä-pə-'gan-də)—Ideas, facts,
or allegations spread deliberately to further
one's cause or damage an opposing cause[1]

oday the word "propaganda" usually holds a negative connotation, even though it was originally used as a term for promoting or "propagating" the Gospel.[2] Today, we think of it more in the negative sense when it is used to harm or injure the truth. We can certainly see that the devil propagates things in an effort to injure the truth of the Gospel. To succeed in this effort, he generally presents truthful facts with key information missing. In essence, he speaks in half-truths. Now, here's the alarming point—half-truths are commonly how we accept much of our information. Don't think so? OK, think of it this way. We often accept "truth" or information without reasonable investigation into its source. In other words, sometimes we don't think about where information comes from, we just think, "Well, it sounds right, so it must be right."

Typically when something is said, we process the information by how it makes us feel at the moment. For example, if it makes us feel warm and cozy, we often respond with an, "Aaaw, isn't that wonderful?" If it makes us angry, we reject it as wrong. Yet the Gospel truth will, at times, evoke anger as it convicts our hearts. Another example is that if the information helps us relate by speaking to our own personal experiences in life, then we allow it to form a portion of our beliefs. If someone tells us something about another person, we're inclined to believe them because their story sounds factual. If a cause or doctrine identifies with some of our own personal dissatisfactions, then we are apt to promote it.

The question is—do we take the time to make sure? Do we investigate the real facts, and are we willing to go against our own feelings and preferences to accept the honest truth? Does what we receive line up with God's measuring stick, the Bible?

I believe it's time to sharpen our discernment in the spirit.

The devil's propaganda comes with a motive to subtly change your thinking. Its intent is to gradually pull you away from godliness in a way that feels *so very* good. The reality is that satan is a master of deception and most commonly uses our personal feelings, experiences, dissatisfactions, and emotions to get us on board with his ideals. He will mix truthful facts into his lies in ways that all seem to identify so closely with our own life. This tactic is used so we feel confident about what he is selling. This is something most of us know but most often forget, and forget repeatedly. Being reminded of this common tendency requires us to take a look at ourselves. We have to consider whether we possess the skills to handle the onslaught of the devil's propaganda that is coming at our lives at an alarming rate.

This book is not just another "watch out for bad stuff" book. It is meant to be a tool—a tool to help Christians learn some key spiritual skills of proper discernment. These skills will work every time and all the time if you embrace them and put them into practice. Now more than ever, we need material that can teach these skills to the Church. We need to be surrounded with it. However, we also need Christian people who are willing to embrace these principles and defend them fervently, even when it's safer to follow the "feel good" trends of the day.

We are living in a very unique time in history. Prophetically, our time is like that of King David when he fought repeated battles against the foreign nations and false gods of his time. Today, our spiritual fight is against the demonic powers that are "foreign" invaders to the Kingdom of light. These spiritual attackers are increasing their efforts, and like David, there are battles on every side. But remember, David had some key men in his corner. In First Chronicles, we find he had, *"The children of Issachar, which were men that had understanding of the times, to know what Israel ought to do..."* (1 Chron. 12:32).

These men had the skills of sharp discernment. They weren't ignorant of the enemies before them, and they had insight into the battle at hand. It is most certain that they didn't gain their sharp skills of discernment by playing ball on sunny afternoons with their old friends in the enemy's campground! No! They didn't hang out with the enemy like many Christians are tricked into doing. Instead, they sharpened their expertise and ability and stayed clear of subtle, "foreign" influences. The name *Issachar* actually means "reward or payback."[3] What an incredible way to get a payback from the devil! With right discernment, we actually have the ability to cut off satan's plans before they ever succeed. There is no greater reward than that.

We need to be like Issachar right now. Today, Christians need to know that the fierce battle at hand wants to destroy their values, steal their purity, and compromise their beliefs. And they need to know the tactics of the carefully calculated spiritual propaganda—custom-made for their own lives—that satan is using to accomplish this goal. We truly need a renewed revelation of these things.

Biblically speaking, it's a dangerous time (see 2 Tim. 3:1). Therefore, it's also time to sharpen our discernment and be willing to stay with God's ways no matter the cost. Doing so is becoming harder with each passing day, and we shouldn't be surprised. The Scriptures prophesied that these days would come.

Let this book be a defining moment for you. May it teach you some key discernment principles, some of which you've heard, some perhaps forgotten, and others that you need to add to your spiritual weaponry. Developing these skills doesn't mean we have to become critical and suspicious individuals, always finding fault with everything. Instead, we can learn to be the most discerning of Christians while remaining teachable and receptive to fresh but sound revelation. All in all, after reading this book, may you become the kind of Christian who sees our modern day with new eyes and who will become skillful with your spiritual tools. May you discern the hour in which we are living and know how to rise above it and finish your God-given race. Most of all, we must decide we will not become the next victim of hell's propaganda.

ENDNOTES

1. "Propaganda," Merriam-Webster Online, http://www.merriam-webster.com/dictionary/propaganda (accessed July 06, 2010).

2. *Ibid.* Etymology.

3. Church of the Great God, "Issachar," Greek/Hebrew Definitions, Strong's http://www.bibletools.org/index.cfm/fuseaction/Lexicon.show/ID (accessed August 20, 2010).

Chapter One

DISCERNING THE LAST DAYS
AND THE GLOBAL MELTDOWN

*This know also, that in the last days perilous
times shall come* (2 Timothy 3:1).

It is easy to get confused these days by all that is available to grab your attention. There are so many new trends, programs, causes, lifestyles, and popular cultures, and our spiritual vision can become cloudy. Of course, today we live in the Information Age. So much information is hurled toward us at almost hurricane wind speeds. There are family members, church friends, neighbors, co-workers, preachers, teachers, the Internet, emails, blogs, newspapers, newsletters, mail, television with hundreds of channels, books, publications, billboards, advertising of every kind, cell phones, and countless other sources. It is so vast, it's become overwhelming to the point where you can hardly take a shower without feeling the need to be near your cell phone or laptop. Now, with the use of Bluetooth devices, we've even attached the online world right to our heads! Obviously, the devil has capitalized on this media generation and has used technology as a primary means of propagating evil, and it is difficult to avoid that influence.

Sadly, many believers have spent little time sharpening their spiritual discernment enough to counter against it. They show little concern for what they should be involved with, listen to, or stand in agreement with. They are ill-prepared to filter through the mass of information coming their way these days and thus end up taking things in according to their emotional feelings. Some people filter out very little at all.

Of course, you cannot avoid every bad piece of information, but overcoming the wrong influences begins with understanding the day we are living in and being able to correctly discern between good and evil. Hebrews says, *"But solid food is for the mature, who by constant use have trained themselves to distinguish good from evil"* (Heb. 5:14 NIV).

You could word it this way: *Mature people train themselves in spiritual discernment because they constantly feed on the right food.* In essence, it will take training to have the kind of spiritual discernment that can stand up in the last days.

We know the days are inherently evil, but if we gain a renewed revelation about it, we might be more careful about what we feed on. By feeding too much on the information of the day, we risk losing discernment. We need our eyes opened in the spirit realm so we don't get swept up with the tide. Without the right discernment, we gradually accept worldly cultures around us because, after all, so many people these days are now "OK with it."

There is more deception now than ever, so it will require a whole new level of discernment as Christians if we are going to weather the times. Our spiritual defenses need to be even more heightened in this hour, because the world is literally on a meltdown.

THE GLOBAL MELTDOWN

The world is on a downward spiral, and the warnings about it are all throughout the New Testament. Jesus talked about it, the early apostles emphasized it, and the Book of Revelation ices the cake on the subject. Whether we realize it or not, sin and evil practices are physically taking their toll on our planet. There is no doubt that a connection exists between the increase in sinful behavior and the natural disasters occurring everywhere.

Not long ago, we were talking to one of our neighbors outside. In the conversation, he brought up the subject of global warming. He was, as most people are, aware that there are many natural catastrophes happening globally, and they are increasing rapidly. So he said, "It must be true about global warming right? Isn't global warming causing all this?"

To this my husband replied with a laugh, "Well, I think our problems are less about global warming than they are about global sinning!"

A key verse about this is found in Romans: *"For we know that the whole creation groaneth and travaileth in pain together until now"* (Rom. 8:22). The context surrounding this verse is speaking of the sufferings of this present world. Literally it means that all that has been created is moaning in unison because it is suffering under a great burden. This world is under a great burden because it is feeling the weight of increasing sin and lawlessness. Think of it like an old house that begins to creak and groan when a strong wind blows. God didn't create the earth to carry sin; He created it to carry His glory.

Sin will eventually destroy everything it touches, and there is no question it is taking its toll on the planet.

The sin problem is not going to get better until Jesus returns in His millennial reign. Until then, things will grow more evil and uncertain in this world. Remember this familiar verse in Matthew which says, *"Because of the increase of wickedness, the love of most will grow cold"* (Matt. 24:12 NIV).

Jesus said wickedness would be on the increase, not on the decrease. Sure, maybe we can argue about global warming in the scientific sense, but we can't argue about it in the spiritual sense. Things are getting hotter! But they are getting "hotter" in the spiritual atmosphere as the world gradually embraces the powers of hell's influence more and more.

STATISTICS DON'T LIE

Some today promote the idea that historically the earth on a wide scale is improving and will continue until whole nations begin turning to God. Statistics prove otherwise. We need a close look at how much the culture has actually declined in a short 30 years in the United States of America alone. There is a pattern that proves that things in the world are not improving overall. It's what the Bible has prophesied, and it should make us think twice about unknowingly joining ranks with the world's way of thinking.

Nearly 20 years ago, William J. Bennett, former Secretary of Education from 1985 to 1988, wrote a compelling article that appeared in the *Wall Street Journal* on March 15, 1993 entitled "Quantifying America's Decline." In the article he provided compelling statistics about the decline of our moral culture.

He shows statistically that from 1960 until 1990, the government dramatically increased social spending from $143.73 billion to $787 billion, yet social behaviors still continued to decline rapidly. During that same period, violent crime increased by 560 percent. There was a 419 percent increase in illegitimate births. Divorce rates quadrupled, and the number of children living in single-parent homes tripled. Shockingly, there was also a 200 percent increase in teen suicide.

He discovered that even though the government made every effort to cure these wrong social behaviors they grew worse. "Social pathologies have not worked," he said. However, probably the most enlightening detail in the article is when he quotes social scientist James Q. Wilson, who said:

> "The powers exercised by the institutions of social control have been constrained, and people, especially young people, have embraced an ethos that values self-expression over self-control."

Plainly said, this means that we are living in a time when human hearts are leaning toward personal pleasure, and they want less to do with moral standards. These numbers were as of the 1990s, but history continues to show that this trend is only growing steadily as time passes.

So where does that leave us today?

A couple of years ago, I was having lunch with a youth pastor in Costa Rica. We were talking about general ministry things and about our experiences in preaching the Gospel. He said to me, "I find it amazing these days how hard and unreceptive people have become to the Gospel message." He didn't live in the United States, but even in his nation the culture was declining. People were accepting more worldly and liberal ideals directly opposed to the Bible in a noticeably resolute fashion. As the Gospel was being preached to them, he discovered that hearts were harder and less open.

Isn't that what Jesus said would take place? Once loving and receptive hearts would become cold and hard, and lawless behavior would rise higher. So, rather than becoming more relaxed, we need to be more alert than ever.

On December 17, 2009, I saw a segment about teen cell phone "sexting" aired on *The O'Reilly Factor*. This is obviously the practice of using phone text messaging technology to send obscene message or photos. Shockingly, it was mentioned on the program that one in three teens today are sexting. Many of these sexting messages are of personal nude photos. Bill O'Reilly brought up the argument that in previous generations we could all think of things that teens did that were perhaps deplorable. However, his guests cited that we have not seen it to the bold forefront magnitude we hear of today. And we certainly wouldn't have heard of such high percentages as one third of teens engaging in such risqué behavior.

Sure, in generations past there were teen pregnancies, drug use, and riotous behavior. However, those of such excesses tended to be more in the background. Thirty-plus years ago, a pregnant teen was looked down upon among most of her peers. It was likely she had to quit high school to avoid public ridicule. Today, she walks the halls of her high school almost as a hero of self-identity and individualism.

Thirty-plus years ago, it was unheard of in high schools to find gay "couples." Homosexuals were virtually non-existent in public discussion or acceptance, and they were never seen among teens. In my high school day, school rules regarding public displays of affection between boys and girls never had to include concerns over homosexual relationships. Today, even *Christian* schools are including policies in their student handbooks against students engaging in public homosexual affection.

On March 11, 2010, the Associated Press released a story about a Mississippi school cancelling the school prom after a female student made efforts to bring her lesbian girlfriend to the high school dance. The young student fought for what she demanded was her "right" to do so, ultimately involving such organizations as the American Civil

Liberties Union (ACLU), whose representatives said, "This is unfair to her. All she's trying to do is assert her rights."[1]

In my high school days, kids fought for the "right" to have pizza in the school lunchroom on Friday! No one would have ever considered the "right" to have a homosexual partner in the high school prom! Something is happening to human hearts when young teens who don't yet have a clear understanding of the reality of any sexual relationship whatsoever, are demanding the "right" to be gay. Hearts are getting harder as time progresses.

In the past, it was more of a common understanding that something was simply wrong with homosexuality. Something was considered strange about two of the same gender having a sexual relationship when their physical anatomy didn't allow them the ability to procreate, causing them to be fully dependent on heterosexuals to support the entire future of life on earth. That alone should be the decisive factor. But human hearts are growing harder to truth. They are ignoring the obvious on purpose to defend their desire to sin.

Something is wrong with the culture when health insurance plans are being created for household pets, but human babies are aborted upon demand by the millions. This was unheard of less than half a century ago.

The world seems to be ignoring the fact that death and bloodshed have become an obsession among not only radical militants and terror groups, but also among modern-day moviegoers and our children. We don't seem to worry when the news reports that kids 10 years of age and younger are committing cold-blooded murder.

Conservationists are saving tons of garbage through recycling efforts in order to "save the planet" while abortion, homicide, genocide, and suicide are mounting in astronomical numbers. There is nothing wrong with recycling, but we cannot stand with the world on something like garbage recycling while we ignore the more detrimental sins of the day.

Statistics don't lie. The world is not improving; it's declining, and here in the United States we actually experience a more softened version of these evils.

In addition to this continual trend of lowering standards, America is becoming less churched. In a study conducted by The Barna Group as far back as 2005, the findings discovered that, in the United States:

> "Despite widespread efforts to increase church at-
> tendance across the nation, the annual survey of
> church attendance conducted by The Barna Group
> shows that one-third of all adults (34%) remain
> 'unchurched.'"[2]

This unchurched group contains many who profess to be active Christians. The report states that, while the number hasn't changed dramatically in the last five years, because of the growing population the number of unchurched adults grows by 1 million people annually.

To further reveal the cultural concerns, the same report also discovered some alarming statistics about the religious beliefs among the same group of unchurched people. They found these beliefs:

> "...That satan is a symbol of evil but not a living
> entity (67% believe this); that if people are good
> enough they can earn their way into Heaven (61%);
> and that Jesus committed sins during His time on
> earth (51%)."[3]

I certainly wonder if these statistics would have been so easily discoverable over 30 years ago. We have to see the time in which we are living.

THE DISEASE OF GRADUAL ACCEPTANCE

The slow and gradual exposure to more crude and immoral living is causing once-discerning Christians to turn a deafened ear. What we once found intolerable, many now realize that seemingly little can be done, so we quit fighting it quite so hard. Dangerously, the more we are exposed to something, the more we get used to it until we no longer see how evil it has become. Then eventually, many just accept it as a part of life, so to speak. Some go the next step of embracing certain ideals altogether.

Jesus prophesied that these times would be upon us. What we need is a new kind of discerning spirit, so we don't gradually accept these worldly ideals or just believe that not everything about them is so terribly wrong. This is where many in the Church are living right now, and there are certain Christians today who seem no longer able to discern the biblical standard of truth.

Several years ago, I was visiting with several ladies over a coffee. One I knew attended a prominent evangelical church in our city and was a professing born-again Christian. She was the mother of teenage boys, and we all got on the subject of raising kids these days. She commented, "Well, I hope if my sons got into a situation with a girl they would make the right choice, but in case they don't, I feel the responsible thing to do as a parent is to make sure they have condoms."

Truthfully, her approach sounds logical and responsible at a glance, but the problem is that her approach as a professing Christian was no different from the secular world. They have replaced teaching godly morals with methods on how to bandage the consequences caused by a lack of morals. Sadly, when I opposed her opinion, she couldn't see my point at all. I suggested instead that we teach our kids the wrongs and painful consequences of having sex outside of marriage.

Unfortunately, you simply cannot bandage all the problems of sexual promiscuity with a condom. While it may *possibly* prevent a pregnancy, it will not mask the many terrible pains that come with sexual promiscuity. And, statistically a condom doesn't even effectively prevent all the problematic things many expect it to prevent.

Years ago, you would be hard-pressed to find any professing Christian taking her approach, but today it's becoming a more common mindset.

Additionally, countless Christians support some of the most violent, off-color, and ungodly forms of entertainment. They dress as close as possible to the world but justify how they can be a good Christian and still present themselves this way. Many have begun to absorb the world's views on everything, from environmental activism to certain radical emphasis on health and fitness, and in many cases liberal political views.

One of the most disconcerting lies being propagated by the world is the new concept of many joined religions and that every religion has its own valid way to God. Now, I don't know of many dedicated *believers* who have fully bought into this idea yet, but that is the problem—they haven't *yet*. Some are already softening to it in the name of "showing love." This new ideal of love and acceptance being heralded on a large scale expects everyone, Christians included, to tolerate and attempt to "understand" all religious groups. Those who don't are considered narrow-minded.

Eventually, some will find certain grounds for agreement with certain tenets of these false religions in order not to make too many waves. It has already begun with the fact that some preachers are apprehensive of saying boldly that Jesus Christ is the only way to God and that eternal punishment is imminent without Him because they fear media controversy.

Most strong Christians still shun the homosexual lifestyle, but many "Christian" groups have softened in their discernment toward it. Gradually they have begun to accept it, because they have become accustomed to its presence in society. Worse is that some are ordaining to ministry—pastors who are proud gays and lesbians! With the assistance of Hollywood movies, television sitcoms, "educational" television, school teachers, and government legislation, the Christian community is becoming slowly accustomed to things such as the existence of homosexual households, acceptance of false religions, and even the defending of near-criminal behavior in many instances.

Christians must realize the fierce battle of our time and sharpen their discernment in the spirit. If we don't, we may not be able to stand in this evil day. Ephesians says:

> *Wherefore take unto you the whole armor of God,*
> *that ye may be able to withstand in the evil day, and*
> *having done all, to stand* (Ephesians 6:13).

The devil has taken his time through the years to gain our "trust" so we will gradually accept things. Slowly but surely, like a terminal illness, he is working us over to receive new mindsets by subtly pulling us away from God's standards. Sometimes it's so subtle that without sharp discernment, we can't tell what is from God and what isn't. Often, Christians live on the fence of uncertainty, afraid of either being too relaxed or overly suspicious and afraid. Some just ignore the need for discernment altogether.

It's time to arm ourselves with the weapon of a discerning spirit and have the right wisdom to resist the deceptions of our day so we don't succumb to this disease of gradual acceptance. This spiritually life-threatening illness will eat away at our very soul if we allow it. We can resist it and overcome it, but it will take all we have in us to stand. That is what Ephesians 6:13 is saying, *"having done all, to stand."*

HOW JESUS TAUGHT DISCERNMENT

It's really pretty simple, but Jesus taught discernment by talking about the times. As we have been discussing, this is such an important principle for having good discernment. However, Jesus didn't just talk about the times so we would get spooky with it. I believe the reason the Church has struggled with filtering through all the information about end-time eschatology is because a lot of time has been spent over-speculating about it. The subject of the end times has been so sensationalized that it is hard to differentiate the true from the false. We've researched how the latest computers have the capacity to support the one-world system or how hand stamps at a theme park might represent the mark! Jesus didn't teach this approach. He taught us to know the signs so we would be better equipped to keep demonic deceptions of the day out of our lives.

Let's first go back to the all-familiar passage of Scripture in Matthew 24. The disciples asked Jesus a specific question: *"...when will this happen, and what will be the sign of Your coming and of the end of the age?"* (Matt. 24:3 NIV).

Jesus is teaching a message on discerning the times in an effort to answer His disciples' question. They wanted to know what signs to look for in order to know when the end was near. He opens with a key statement: *"Take heed that no man deceive you"* (Matt. 24:4). Jesus' initial answer was that we pay close attention so that *we* do not fall into the trap of deception as the end approaches. He admonishes them to not be fearful and to endure in righteousness. He was teaching them the evils of the day so they would be sharp in their discernment and not fall into deception.

Notice the words *"take heed"* in this verse. Really, it means to take a deep look into something. Spiritually speaking, we could say it means we need to get a spiritual perception or prophetic insight.

What we really need is a revelation from the Holy Spirit so that we can look at our day through God's eyes.

This is something we cannot do by listening to primetime news all the time. We simply cannot take in constant input from the secular culture and expect to receive God's perspective on things. Deception can first be avoided when we work hard to avoid the sources from which deception comes. Some might say, "Well, what is wrong with the nightly news?" In short, nothing is wrong with taking a brief look at today's events. But something is wrong when your source of input from the world's perspective outweighs your time listening to God's perspective.

It is like exercise. What you put your energy into is what will dominate your life. If you work out every day, you will get fit. If you lay on the couch eating potato chips every day, you will suffer the results. The same is true in the things of the spirit, and this is what Jesus was talking about in Matthew 24:4. Pay attention or put in the time it takes to avoid deception, because in this day deception is out there and ready to invade your thinking.

From there, Jesus revealed several traps of deception that we have to discern as the end approaches. Many people are aware of the signs of the end times from a global perspective, but we have to take it a step further and watch how these things might try to seep into our own lives.

SIX TRAPS OF DECEPTION

From Matthew 24, Jesus taught several deceptive traps that lie in wait in the last days, and He gave us keys to avoid them.

1. *False anointing will be prominent.*

"Many shall come in My name, saying, I am Christ; and shall deceive many" (Matt. 24:5). The word *Christ* in the Greek means

"anointed." We can conclude here that many will act or pretend to be "anointed." This will confuse many people who are not sharp in their discernment. It is happening a lot these days. There are many things that pretend to be from God but are not.

How do we avoid them? *Take heed or watch for them.* Ask yourself if it lines up with Scripture. But even beyond that—is the character of the one who is speaking godly and proven? Don't become a ruthless critic, but ask yourself some key questions. Paul told Timothy, *"But continue thou in the things which thou hast learned and hast been assured of, knowing of whom thou hast learned them"* (2 Tim. 3:14).

In other words, remember the good sources from which you have gained your godly foundation and stick with them. Don't just jump into something that sounds "powerful" and drop all you have learned thus far. Keep your foothold in what you have learned from the Bible and from anointed and proven ministers or people over the years.

2. *There will be many wars and much talk about war.*

"And ye shall hear of wars and rumors of wars: see that ye be not troubled..." (Matt. 24:6). Jesus was warning us that the last days will contain many great conflicts. Yes, there will be countless national wars, but on a smaller scale the day will also be marked by strife and fighting. This characteristic is prevalent today, isn't it? To stay aware of the day we live in, we must know that war and fighting will be on the rise. Warfare, terrorism, gang violence, divorce, and hatred will all be part of it.

So how do we avoid it? Don't get caught up in the fighting spirit of the day. Stay away from reasons to argue and get into strife. When we get angry, we only open ourselves up for deception. We lower our discerning immune system, so to speak. Anger and fighting can make us do many things we will later be sorry for. We lose all proper reason under the influence of anger.

Some Christians have fallen into the trap of criticizing their fellow believers. Sure, we may not all agree on every tidbit of doctrine or belief, but when we don't agree, we cannot become the next "soapbox" believer who is out to emphasize fault with all the wrong in Christianity. Instead, when at all possible, be a bridge builder and a peacemaker in a day of war and strife. Don't be an Internet blogging critic or a church troublemaker just because some in the Body of Christ are different than you. Instead, discern how you need to approach *your own* personal Christianity and love your brothers and sisters in Christ at the same time. After all, they are devoted to the same Jesus you are! (See Luke 9:49-56.)

3.   Natural disaster will be paramount.

"...And there shall be famines, and pestilences, and earthquakes, in diverse places. All these are the beginning of sorrows" (Matt. 24:7-8). Of course, it isn't hard to be reminded of the times as we see natural disasters all around us today. We can see the sorrow on television as people lose their homes or loved ones to fires, floods, and earthquakes. Nature in an uproar causes a lot of human pain. However, Jesus gave us a key anecdote as Christians, and that is to stay in the joy of the Lord.

When the large earthquake happened in Haiti early in 2010, I heard a report on Christian radio that in the immediate days to follow some Christians got together and started praising God in the streets and singing. What were they doing? They were replacing sorrow with joy by praising the Lord.

Sure anyone can feel sad when they've experienced a great tragedy. However, there are demons attached to sorrow that want us to fall into the deceptions that accompany grief and sorrow. They want us to go from one bad day or negative experience into a cycle of stress and hurt until we eventually become trapped by depression and fear. From there, they want us to blame God and lose our trust in Him.

Several months ago we were flying into Houston. As we approached the airport I saw all the freeways winding around each other filled with traffic. I had been on those exact freeways years before in a car and remembered the traffic being overwhelming! It was almost terrifying! But from the airplane those same cars looked like toys. I felt as if I could pick each car up with my fingers and move it however I wanted. From up there, everything felt conquerable. Jesus said, *"Let not your heart be troubled..."* (John 14:1). In other words, just don't allow it! Let the supernatural power of God's joy and peace help you overcome the sorrows of the last days. Command your mind to focus on the goodness of God over your own hurts and disappointments. When you do, you will see more clearly in the spirit and keep God's perspective of earth in view.

4. Persecution will intensify.

> *Then shall they deliver you up to be afflicted, and shall kill you: and ye shall be hated of all nations for My name's sake. And then shall many be offended, and shall betray one another, and shall hate one another* (Matthew 24:9-10).

This makes us painfully aware that the world will take on a new level of intolerance for the people of God. They will find Christianity more distasteful and will do all they can to silence its influence. In some places, Christians are literally killed or imprisoned. In the United States, we find Christian rights continually being choked out by litigation, legislation, and protests.

When this happens, what did Jesus say would take place? Many believers would turn on their own brothers and sisters. They would stumble and give in until they eventually betrayed the very people and principles they once defended. Intense persecution can make some go against their long-lived standards.

Jesus had an amazing understanding of this human tendency found in Mark 3:20-21 and 31-35. The story is that Jesus was preaching and was pressed upon so much by the multitudes that He and his apostles couldn't even stop to eat. His family heard of it and seeing His extreme commitment to ministry, they felt He had gone a little too far. In verse 21, they even said that Jesus had lost His mind, so they decided to go and grab hold of Him! When they arrived, they stood outside of the house where Jesus was ministering and called for Him. When the people heard it, they told Jesus that His mother and family were outside. Apparently knowing their intent, Jesus said, *"Who is My mother, or My brethren?"*(See Mark 3:33.) He then looked around at all the people He had been ministering to and said, *"...Behold My mother and My brethren! For whosoever shall do the will of God, the same is My brother, and My sister, and mother"* (Mark 3:34-35).

Seems a pretty bold statement in front of one's mother, don't you think? Of course, Jesus isn't advocating being rude, but He was saying that when last-days persecution heats up, it requires us to examine where our loyalties are. Can we choose the Kingdom over boisterous relatives? Can we stay with the Bible when co-workers and job expectations demand something else? If not, we will be like those Jesus mentions in Matthew 24:10. We will potentially become offended at the ideals of the Gospel and with those who defend it.

We resist the deceptions that increase with persecution by making decisive choices with our loyalties. Our closest alliances must be with those who are dedicated to the Kingdom of God. Sure, we may not always agree with fellow church members or our pastor, but if they are pushing us toward God, stick by them. They may save your life.

5. *False prophets and predictors will increase.*

"And many false prophets shall rise, and shall deceive many" (Matt. 24:11). False prophets don't have to be strange individuals that go

around in long white robes, carrying tambourines and marrying multiple wives. Actually, the New Testament has more to say about false teachers than false prophets, and scripturally false prophets were marked less by what they prophesied than by what they taught. They were held accountable more for their ungodly character and false teaching. My husband, Hank, wrote a wonderful book on the characteristics of false prophets called *The Revealer of Secrets*.[4] I would encourage you to read it.

Here I want you to see that Jesus was warning us of those who would lead us astray through their false teachings. We will cover in-depth later in this book how to recognize dangerous false teaching, but the first thing we must note is that it will be everywhere.

These false teachers don't have to come dressed as a preacher either. Usually that is the only place we look for them. Sadly, some Christians trust the news anchor more than most ministers. We are more critical of television preachers than the secular talk show hosts. The first place we need to look for false prophets is in the world's camp!

The devil is attempting to propagate prophecy to you every day through the television and the Internet. Sure, dangerous flu viruses might exist, but the devil will prophesy the fear of them to you every day through the media until the only voice you hear is from these sources. Eventually, you believe the godless scientist over the God of the Bible. The devil will prophesy to you through scantily-dressed women parading across the most popular sports channels, but we ignore the danger of these "prophecies."

We listen carefully to the countless prescription drug commercials that promise near-miracle cures with little proof of their effectiveness. Even with lots of potentially harmful effects, we buy them with our life's savings. We carefully tune into the "experts" on the economy so we can decide how to plan our financial future and know what to expect about our employment in the upcoming days.

You can see how we listen freely to the prophets of the world, and the false propagations they make often go undetected by our ears.

Jesus said false prophets would deceive many a Christian. Why? Because we perk our ear to the places they are speaking most. I believe there are far fewer reasons to fear false prophets in the pulpits of good churches and on Christian television than from the world's venues. Yet most Christians point the finger of accusation toward the falseness in the ministry. Sure, there are false prophets there too, but be far more aware of them from the world's camp. That is where they deceive people the most.

6. Sin will abound and increase.

"And because iniquity shall abound, the love of many shall wax cold" (Matt. 24:12). As I showed earlier in this chapter, we know a drive toward sin is prevalent in the world more than ever before. We can't avoid what is all around us. The world loves sin and will often applaud sinful people (see Rom. 1:32). In this increased sin environment, Jesus said hearts would become hardened. They become less willing to be helpful, considerate, and mannerly. You can see that today just by the way people drive their cars! If they are late to work, they may run you off the road if you seem to be in their way.

To resist the sin environment, we need to simply realize that we cannot be friends with the world. John writes:

> *Love not the world, neither the things that are in the world. If any man love the world, the love of the Father is not in him. For all that is in the world, the lust of the flesh, and the lust of the eyes, and the pride of life, is not of the Father, but is of the world* (1 John 2:15-16).

Too many Christians these days are too aligned with the world. They spend all of their time going to movies, shopping malls, and sporting events. They love television and live for the latest fashion craze. They live to own all the latest electronics so they can stay more connected to their worldly loves. Many are more dedicated to their secular music and favorite Hollywood star than to Jesus. It's evident by how they spend their time.

While there is nothing wrong with a controlled amount of television or going to the occasional movie, something is wrong when Christians can quote movie lines more than Bible verses. We are fooling ourselves thinking that we won't get entangled in the world's sinful ways with these actions.

Here is another compelling thought. When Jesus said people's love would grow cold because of the increase of sin, it is mostly that people's love for *Him* would grow cold. Sure, our love toward others will decrease, but so does our passionate love for the Lord. By spending a little less time in the presence of the world's influences—especially through media—and more time in God's presence, you will keep your defenses up against the sins of the day.

Decades of statistics have proven that the world is not improving. Therefore, we need to be watchful and discerning Christians. No, we shouldn't live in unnecessary fear and suspicion, and we do need to love people in order to reach them with the Gospel. But we cannot come into alliance with their actions.

As we bring this chapter to a close, let me encourage you with this verse: *"Be on your guard; stand firm in the faith; be men of courage; be strong"* (1 Cor. 16:13 NIV). The earth may be in turmoil as the last days grow closer, but for discerning believers, we can stand the test to avoid falling into the evils of the day!

ENDNOTES

1. Deepti Hajela, "Lesbian Miss. Teen Is Marshal at NYC Pride March," Yahoo! News, http://news.yahoo.com/s/ap/us_lesbian _prom_date (accessed July 6, 2010).

2. The Barna Group, "One in Three Adults Is Unchurched," Barna Update, http://www.barna.org/barna-update/article/ 5-barna-update/182-one-in-three-adults-is-unchurched (accessed July 7, 2010).

3. *Ibid*. Religious Beliefs.

4. Hank Kunneman, *The Revealer of Secrets* (Lake Mary, FL: Charisma House, 2009).

Chapter Two

Lessons From Balaam: How to Recognize the Spirit of Compromise

Fire tests the purity of silver and gold, but the Lord tests the heart (**Proverbs 17:3 NLT**).

He was known for his mysterious insight into the realm of unseen spiritual things. His reputation for having some kind of special power apparently preceded him, and this time it captured the attention of a national leader who was in a very desperate predicament. The leader felt it was his only hope to avoid economic collapse. So, it was time to call for him—that well-known diviner who came from the town of Pethor.

You probably already know this story, but the Bible uses the life of this false prophet named Balaam to teach us some of the greatest lessons about discernment.

Let's begin with some brief history into the prophet Balaam, found in Numbers 22. Although the Bible refers to him as a prophet, he was *not* a prophet of the Lord (see 2 Pet. 2:15-16). The term *prophet* was likely used for "false prophet," since the Bible also refers to the prophets of Baal as "prophets" (see 1 Kings 18:22). Most historical accounts refer to Balaam as a diviner or soothsayer. Additionally, his name actually means "not of the people." From this you could derive that he was not part of the children of Israel.

The story begins as Israel approaches Moab near the end of their 40 years in the wilderness. They had already defeated two powerful kings, and Moab probably knew of their victories. However, it is likely that Israel didn't intend to invade Moab because they were descendants of Lot, and Israel was instructed not to take their land (see Deut. 2:9). It was more probable that their presence was an economic intrusion (see Num. 22:3). The king probably feared their sheer size and numbers would overwhelm their economic stability, as he indicates, *"This horde is going to lick up everything around us, as an ox licks up the grass of the field"* (Num. 22:4 NIV).

So Balak, the king of Moab, aligns with the leaders of Midian and calls for Balaam, asking him to place a curse on Israel. He must have believed that only a spiritual curse would get them out of his region. Certainly, after they had defeated two kings, Moab didn't dare to attack them!

Balaam must have had a reputation for spiritual channeling or the king of Moab would not have known to seek for him, and the king must have believed that Balaam had the legitimate power to do channeling (see Num. 22:5-7). We also see that when the king sent his messengers to speak to Balaam, they carried with them money to pay for his services: "...*taking with them the fee for divination...*" (Num. 22:7 NIV). It must have been understood, if you were going to seek someone for access into the spirit realm, that you paid them, just as someone might pay a palm reader today. This proves that they were obviously not seeking a true prophet of the Lord!

So why then *did* Balaam inquire of the Lord? Some believe it would have been normal for a soothsayer to first make some kind of contact with the "god" (actually a demonic power) protecting the people he was dealing with. The assumption by diviners was to seek some kind of permission. However, in this case Balaam was not just dealing with any other god! He was dealing with Israel, whose God was Jehovah!

It is also apparent that Balaam knew who the God of Israel was, as he indicates by saying, "...*I will bring you word again, as the Lord shall speak unto me...*" (Num. 22:8). The word he used for the Lord here was actually *Jehovah*. Either he had already heard previous stories, or he did some research to find out.

As the story goes, we learn that even though Balaam attempted to curse Israel, he couldn't! When his mouth tried to speak a curse over the people, he could only speak a blessing. He realized very quickly that he wasn't going to get past this particular God! He tried several times to curse the people to no avail.

Most of all, we remember the part where the angel of the Lord stood in Balaam's way as he went with the king's men to go place the curse. The angel caused his donkey to stumble, and when Balaam got angry and hit the animal, the angel caused Balaam's donkey to speak! Balaam must have been accustomed to strange spiritual occurrences, because he actually answered the donkey back!

Finally, in Numbers 24:1-2 when Balaam realized that God wouldn't allow a curse to come upon Israel and that God was pleased to bless them, he quit his magic enchantments and actually began to prophesy by the Spirit of the Lord. He finally gets the real revelation that an unbreakable blessing and protection rested upon these people. At that moment it seems he got a personal revelation of the power of the one true God! The Bible says his eyes were opened.

This shows who we are in Christ. Just like Israel, we are blessed! Ephesians says, *"Blessed be the God and Father of our Lord Jesus Christ, who hath blessed us with all spiritual blessings in heavenly places in Christ"* (Eph. 1:3). Even when Balaam tried to curse the people of God, he couldn't because there was a shield of protection over them. That same protection exists over every Christian too. Balaam told the king, *"...the Lord their God is with them; the shout of the King is among them"* (Num. 23:21 NIV). It is certain that all the shouting and worship to God in the camp of Israel prevented evil from coming. There is something about human shouts, decrees, and speaking words of faith that settle things in the realm of the spirit. Words spoken aloud can help you make decisions, intimidate demons, and set the atmosphere. Surely, part of Israel's blessing was because of their shout. It prevented evil.

ENEMY ACCESS

Balaam soon gave up the idea of placing a curse on the children of Israel and went home. Look here at Numbers 24: *"And Balaam rose up, and went and returned to his place: and Balak also went his way"* (Num. 24:25). But look at the very next verse:

> *And Israel abode in Shittim, and the people began to commit whoredom with the daughters of Moab. And they called the people unto the sacrifices of their gods: and the people did eat, and bowed down to their gods. And Israel joined himself unto Baalpeor: and the anger of the Lord was kindled against Israel"* (Numbers 25:1-3).

Sure, Balaam had been blocked from cursing the people, but suddenly immediately following his attempts the children of Israel began to worship the false gods of Moab and Midian: *"Israel joined himself unto Baalpeor."* Baalpeor was the same false god Baal we read of throughout the Bible. In this case the name promotes him as the deity of worship in the city of Peor.

Baal's name gives a clue to why the children of Israel sinned. *Baalpeor* means "lord of the gap." A gap is a breach, crack, or opening. It seems that there was some kind of crack in the defenses of Israel that caused them to compromise, leaving them vulnerable to enemy access.

Satan and the hoards of hell are opportunists that look for a small opening into which they can squeeze their evil influences into our lives. They look for the weak areas and the places where our motives may not be aligned just right. They are hunting for areas of compromise in your heart which they can use to get you to lower your defenses in the spirit. Then they use subtle influences against you and repeatedly bombard your mind in those weak areas. Demons don't mind chipping away a little bit at a time and will use whatever "crack" you give them. By telling you what you want to hear, they are hoping you won't notice these subtle influences until you slowly compromise your standards.

Compromise dulls a discerning spirit. This is because if there is a small compromise or "gap" in your heart you will quit looking at something through spiritual eyes. In order to continue fulfilling the desire for it, you perhaps justify it, try to get Scripture to support your indulgence, or get others to agree with you. Many believers even quit listening to godly preachers, teachers, and counselors and start listening only to the voices that tell them what they want to hear. That is why many Christians would rather listen to the secular psychologist on television than hear the voice of their pastor. They want to feel good about those "gaps" that they know are in their hearts.

Many years ago, a couple came to us for marriage counseling. Actually, we don't spend much time doing marriage counseling.

Typically, we provide other events or resources for couples to improve their marriage. Truthfully, all the best counseling in the world cannot help unless they are both willing to be doers of the Word of God. People who refuse to do the basic things—such as being considerate, forgiving, or living responsibly—will not make good marriage partners or even good Christians.

In this case, we gave the couple the best biblical insight we knew. The problem was neither of them wanted to be consistent in their godly behavior. Some months later, we heard that they had signed up with an out-of-town secular marriage professional, even spending money for travel. They felt they needed more, and perhaps they *did* need more. The problem was they didn't want to do the basic truths of Scripture.

Some people always want something else but never want to do what the Bible tells them. They are always looking for something new that supports their unwillingness to address private compromises. As a result, they quit discerning things correctly.

If we are always looking for the things we want to hear instead of what we need to hear, because of compromise we will lose our discernment and become susceptible to enemy access. This is what Second Timothy says:

> *For the time will come when men will not put up with sound doctrine. Instead, to suit their own desires, they will gather around them a great number of teachers to say what their itching ears want to hear. They will turn their ears away from the truth and turn aside to myths* (2 Timothy 4:3-4 NIV).

It is no question that this is what happened to the children of Israel. Balaam influenced them to worship Baal by offering something that perked their interest, and they fell for it.

Historically, Baal was considered to provide sexual fertility, and often in ancient days many of these false religions would propagate very promiscuous sexual freedom. Israel was always prone to lustful compromise, making them open to easily receive this type of false religion. Undoubtedly, that is what Balaam offered them—sexual freedom. How convenient it would have been to "justify" their immoral behavior by saying it was a religious practice! In no time the people were having lewd relations with the Midianites. The Bible says they became *joined* to Baal. Balaam simply encouraged them to give in and embrace what they really wanted.

> *Behold, these caused the children of Israel, through the counsel of Balaam, to commit trespass against the Lord in the matter of Peor...* (Numbers 31:16).

Since Balaam couldn't curse the people, he used the methods of teaching and giving subtle advice to bring them down. It didn't even take a witchcraft curse. All it took was some creative manipulation to encourage them to relax and go with their feelings.

SELF-DISCERNMENT

For Israel, the compromise of their own hearts made them lose their discernment so they lowered their standard. Listening to someone who supported their lustful feelings was all it took. They threw aside all checks and balances.

As Christians, we must check our hearts if we want to have the proper spiritual safeguards. The most discerning Christian is the one who can first discern themselves. Sometimes we think the only real discernment we need is for everything else, but we forget to look inside. Your ability to discern between the truth and a lie will be more accurate when you are willing to do a personal heart check. Spend less time looking at what is wrong with others and start with yourself.

Typically in the Body of Christ we love to "discern" all the wrong doctrines, sins of others, and errors of preachers. This has its proper place, but people get so caught up in that small portion of discernment and do little to discern their own heart motives. That is why they get offtrack and critical.

The devil has a much smaller chance of propagating lies to you if you can take an honest examination of your heart. That is why God always looks at our hearts. He knows what is on the inside is what will make you. Look at Proverbs: *"Fire tests the purity of silver and gold, but the Lord tests the heart"* (Prov. 17:3 NLT).

What does the Lord do? He tests our hearts with fire. He will sometimes cause divine disruptions in our lives to see how we respond. A godly response shows spiritual maturity, while a bad response reveals sin and compromise. No, God doesn't put evil on us through methods such as sickness and tragedy. Those things come from the devil who comes to kill (see John 10:10). But sometimes God will do things like remove you from your current job to reposition you for something else. He will use the process to bring the hidden motives to the surface, where we recognize and deal with them.

Take on the attitude that you are willing to become a discerning believer by discerning your own heart first. It will make you more accurate as a discerning Christian.

TRAPS OF COMPROMISE

It is important to look at some specifics on what Balaam taught the people. It was more than just tempting them with sexual sin. He gave the people what they wanted to hear. Amazingly, we will find that this same trap causes many Christians to lose their discernment and drop their most treasured principles. If gone undetected in our hearts, we can begin to view situations and circumstances with cloudy vision. Then we think we have the right perspective when in fact there are some huge gaps and breaches.

Look at a message to the Church of Pergamos:

> *But I have a few complaints against you. You tolerate some among you whose teaching is like that of Balaam, who showed Balak how to trip up the people of Israel. He taught them to sin by eating food offered to idols and by committing sexual sin* (Revelation 2:14 NLT).

From both this verse and from Second Peter we can find some of what Balaam encouraged them to do.

> *Forsaking the right way, they have gone astray, having followed the way of Balaam, the son of Beor, who loved the wages of unrighteousness; but he received a rebuke for his own transgression, for a mute donkey, speaking with a voice of a man, restrained the madness of the prophet. These are springs without water and mists driven by a storm, for whom the black darkness has been reserved. For speaking out arrogant words of vanity they entice by fleshly desires, by sensuality, those who barely escape from the ones who live in error, promising them freedom while they themselves are slaves of corruption; for by what a man is overcome, by this he is enslaved. For if, after they have escaped the defilements of the world by the knowledge of the Lord and Savior Jesus Christ, they are again entangled in them*

*and are overcome, the last state has become worse for
them than the first* (2 Peter 2:15-20 NASB).

Look closely at Second Peter 2:20. It's talking about Christians
who were on fire for the Lord and lived holy lives in the beginning
of their walk with God. But they got caught up again with the sinful
practices of the world. It says they were *"again entangled in them and
are overcome."*

An easier way of understanding what it means to get entangled
would simply be to say they got too involved with it. The reason many
good Christian people get sold lies by the devil is because they spend
too much time putting worldly things into their hearts.

Maybe it started by simply watching a little too much political
television until eventually they found less time for the Bible. Then
the secular information started changing their views. Or maybe it
was too much time spent running their children to Little League on
Sunday until finally they reasoned that church wasn't all that important and perhaps less necessary than they once believed. It could have
been too many extra hours at the office that left them little time for
God and family that finally caused their life to fall apart. You can see
how these little, seemingly-innocent compromises caused them to lose
discernment and eventually led to a life away from God. *Compromise
in your heart leads to loss of discernment, which always leads to sin.*

Here are some of the compromises Balaam taught from the
verses above.

SELFISH MOTIVES

When we become too focused on self, we find ourselves wanting
things we don't need or shouldn't have.

I have known countless young, single Christians who really want
to get married. For a season, they spend time using their faith, asking

God for the right mate, and so on. However, as time passes they continue to focus too excessively on the need to get married. For some it's all they think about until it opens the door to selfish motives. Eventually, the devil capitalizes on their overwhelming desire and sends them somebody usually very wrong for them. Typically it's someone worldly, abusive, or just irresponsible. By now their heart has compromised, making them less discerning about whom they choose. For some it finally comes down to taking anyone who will give them notice. Eventually, they go back to a worldly lifestyle altogether in order to keep the relationship they've gotten involved with.

The verses above say that there are those who come along that will *entice with fleshly desires.* They will prey on what is already in your heart, like Balaam did to Israel. He capitalized on their own lusts, and they dropped their discernment so they could run out and have what they really wanted.

Here are some of the most common examples of selfish motives.

MONEY AND COVETOUSNESS

This is a love of money as the Bible says in First Timothy 6:10. Both poor and rich people can have a love for money. Some who have spent much of their lives with very little can become so consumed with doing "whatever it takes" to get ahead they lose sight (discernment) of what is important. They quit tithing, they work too much, they quit on God and church, or they are willing to steal and do sinful things in order to make a buck. Second Peter 2:15 that we read above says they *"loved the wages of unrighteousness."* That means they loved to earn money by doing wrong. Again, it's what Balaam encouraged Israel to do.

Some people just spend too much time desiring material pleasure, so the devil gives them plenty of ways to spend their temptation. They constantly dream of that big vacation. They feel life would be different once they get their dream home. They will over-extend their means to have that snazzy car. Yet the Kingdom of God is at the bottom of their list.

If an excessive focus of material things is in your heart, repent of it. Sow a financial seed into the Kingdom of God. Make a fresh commitment not to allow materialism to come between you and the Lord.

SELF-PROMOTION

Another selfish motive is the need for self-promotion. Some overly desire recognition and personal achievement. Sure, there is nothing wrong with wanting a reward for hard work and feeling the normal human need for people to appreciate you. But when it becomes a constant goal, it gets out of line. We also find in our same passage above that those who desire to promote themselves spend time, *"speaking out arrogant words of vanity"* (2 Pet. 2:18 NASB). This is what gives birth to pride. They always want the topic of conversation to be about them.

Always wanting the next big "break" or the next deal is also a form of self-promotion and will alter godly priorities. Advance because you want to do something for the Lord, not to promote self. People who get caught up in self-promotion will end up hurting other people too. They will do unethical things on the job to get noticed by the boss and even perhaps mistreat co-workers. Perhaps they will ignore the needs of their children because they are too busy working for something they want to achieve. Many preachers also get caught up in self promotion and forget their true ministry purpose which is to promote the Kingdom of God.

As you pursue goals, ask yourself if an excessive desire for self-promotion exists in your heart. James says, *"Wherefore he saith, God resisteth the proud, but giveth grace unto the humble"* (James 4:6). No matter how much you may feel the need to pursue your dream, avoid the pride of self-promotion. Ask yourself if you are overstepping any ethical boundaries in order to gain an advantage. Decide if there are things you say in order to garner praise. Be confident in who you are, and as you pursue better things, do it to give glory to Jesus.

PERSONAL FREEDOM

This is when people don't want any form of rules except those that they feel work within their own habits. If they love to sleep in, they don't want to attend church on Sunday morning. If they have a problem with gluttony, perhaps fasting isn't their thing, and they will disagree with any preacher who teaches and promotes the benefits of fasting. They don't want any boundaries that make them strive for righteousness. Again, our same passage says, *"...promising them freedom while they themselves are slaves of corruption; for by what a man is overcome, by this he is enslaved"* (2 Peter 2:19 NASB).

We can't believe that there is any liberty outside of godly boundaries. We are losing discerning insight if we believe otherwise. Many today don't want a pastor to confront issues from the pulpit because they don't want anyone putting stringent rules on them. Striving for personal freedom in a way that liberates you from the rule of Christ will ruin you. Many quit discerning accurately because of it. There are rules to serving Jesus, referred to in Scripture as the *"law of Christ"* (see Gal. 6:2).

I once heard a preacher pray this prayer: "Lord, keep me on a short leash." They were asking the Lord to help them keep from straying away in the area of excessive personal freedoms. It isn't right to be bound to fanatical legalisms, but it is good to be bound to the Lord and a godly lifestyle.

WORLDLY CRAVING

Balaam also capitalized on the worldly cravings that were in the hearts of the children of Israel. Some people are less concerned about selfish motives, but rather have an addiction to worldliness. They simply love all the colors and lights of the world. They just can't seem to break away from everything the world has to offer in terms of friends, lifestyles, and ideas. In fact, they will even defend them tooth and toenail.

I remember many years ago a Christian recommending to us a movie. The movie was about a man who was to be paid one million dollars to have an affair with another man's wife. Now, I don't know about you, but the entire premise of the movie is about as anti-godly as you can get. I wouldn't watch it in a million years, much less for a million dollars! There are far too many Christians these days who support Hollywood principles over godly principles.

Some attend movies with promiscuous themes. They wait for the latest crime scene investigation murder-thriller, or for some reason they think that certain sci-fi films are a good source for learning godly principles. I simply can't see it. They will almost treat these things as their profound method of personal enlightenment. They quote lines from them and give them more time and credence than the Bible.

Some will defend and mimic the lifestyles of their favorite television stars or athletes. They love to read all the celebrity gossip. They want to act like them or at least dress like them. Women's clothes are getting tighter these days, while young men mimic the styles of gangs and gothic rockers.

A worldly craving is dangerous and will annihilate true spiritual discernment. With it you will eventually exchange your insight from the Holy Spirit in order to fit in with those who entice you.

WORLDLY FRIENDSHIPS

I have already been alluding to this truth somewhat, but I do want to encourage readers that we cannot make our best friends those who are of the world. Some of these worldly friendships can exist right in our spirit-filled, tongue-talking churches! Yet they live on the edge of compromise.

During our years of pastoring, I have realized more than ever the truth of the old saying, "Birds of a feather will flock together." I'm amazed at how many people who are rebellious against pastors will find each other. People who have a problem with this or that will always find the other person in the congregation with the same concerns.

There are also those who tend to strike up friendships with people with their same bad habits. For example, people trying to overcome addiction become friends with other addicts. Now, there isn't a thing wrong with trying to gain a friend for accountability and moral support. However, in my ministry experience this setup doesn't always work. Sometimes they want to hang with others struggling in the same areas so if they slip they feel there is someone who "understands" them. They use it to feel OK about their sin. Truthfully, we don't always need someone to relate. Rather, we need someone who puts the fire under us and saves our backside. In light of eternity, we probably need people who can't relate to us in our compromises at all!

Making close worldly alliances makes us an enemy of the Lord. That is what the Bible says in James. *"...Know ye not that friendship with the world is enmity with God? Whosoever therefore will be a friend of the world is the enemy of God"* (James 4:4). Avoid worldly friendships. That doesn't mean you turn a callous heart to the lost or people who are struggling, it just means you don't make the people of the world or even carnal Christians your closest relationships or allow them to influence you. Build friendships with Christians who push you on to godliness, aren't afraid to call you on the carpet, and who will keep you straight—no excuses!

SEXUAL IMMORALITY

Some people's problem with worldly cravings is sexual. Usually these people are those who struggle with some of the things we've already mentioned. They hang with worldly people, they watch worldly television, and they read news articles and columns they should probably avoid. Sexual immorality has the ability to destroy more than most other fleshly sins and is a root cause to many other sinful behaviors. Many lives have been destroyed because of it.

I was never Catholic, but I once heard someone quote Pope John Paul II on television. When asked his opinion on the issue of sexual activity outside of marriage, he responded to say something profound. While it may not be an exact quote, to my memory it was along these lines: "All I know is that countless lives would suffer a great deal less hurt and turmoil without it."

Isn't that true? Think of all the children that might not be products of divorce if their parents had remained faithful. How many countless people might not be sitting alone today with broken hearts and feeling dirty and rejected, had some form of promiscuity not been a part of their lives?

Sexual lust is controlled by taking in the right spiritual food. Feeding on the Bible, worshiping the Lord, having the right friends, and listening to faith-filled preaching will naturally bring any fleshy behaviors under control. Decide you will do whatever necessary to take authority over sexual compromise in your heart. If it's a serious problem for you, become accountable to somebody. Look at it in the light of eternity, and don't allow its deceptive clutches to kill your discernment.

SECULAR IDEALISM

Another key area when it comes to dealing with the compromise of worldly cravings is taking on secular ideals. Many Christians do it unknowingly. The prevalent problem area for this is with politics. We have almost developed a political idolatry in the United States these days. We have almost subconsciously begun thinking that we need the right elected officials in office if the Lord is going to have any chance of displaying His power. Therefore, we praise the political leaders we believe in with almost blind faith. We treat them as a "messiah" of sorts, expecting them to keep our world straight so we can go happily on with our lives.

Many Christians quit using biblical discernment because they want to stand behind a leader who promises to fix their personal problems. As a result, they will start to take on certain secular principles in order to stand with their candidate.

Truthfully, we have to remind ourselves that much of the political world today is entirely secular. This is true in every political party. If we put too much credence into a secular system just because it speaks to our personal campaigns, we might lose sight of the more eternal issues. Again, these heart compromises make us dull of spiritual discernment.

Remember that secular ideals—no matter how beautifully they are painted and no matter what party of governmental persuasion they come from—are still secular. Even though our nation was originally founded with godly principles in mind, today our government is steadily becoming more secular. We need to remind ourselves of this fact.

Once again bringing in Second Peter, we find they were *"forsaking the right way, they have gone astray..."* (2 Pet. 2:15 NASB). Some secular views may have truth to them, but we must be guarded and realize that in the end we are first defenders of the Gospel. Paul said, *"...I am set for the defense of the Gospel"* (Phil. 1:17). Simply said, make sure secular ideals are not your focus and first priority.

RELIGIOUS TRADITION

Lastly, if we recall back to the compromises that Balaam taught, we find the word *"doctrine"* being used in Revelation 2:14, which we read earlier. This means there was some sort of deliberate teaching and training taking place. The people were becoming his students.

We also find that included in Balaam's doctrine was that he taught the people sin, which included idolatry and fornication. More than likely he gave them reason to believe that their actions were justifiable because there was "religious" credence to them.

Many claiming to be Christian today will stand behind certain religious traditions so they can keep certain lifestyles. Some will cite that they are of such-and-such denomination because they don't want any kind of Christianity that forces them to be too radical.

Hitting closer to home for many Pentecostals and Charismatics, we have those who only want church on their terms. If the worship isn't a certain way, they can't flow. They want an experience that is familiar to their religious experience. However, I have learned that the things of God are always progressive, and they go far beyond my limited lifetime experience.

Recently, I watched a video of some of the old Charismatic 1950s tent revivals and healing meetings. These were with many of the great ministries many of us in Charismatic circles have heralded and loved. I was surprised by the delivery of some. The preachers were very dramatic in almost the old news styles of the time. I felt for a moment like I was viewing a narrative from an old black and white television superhero program! Yet I knew the anointing was there and people were getting healed. Today, television preaching is a world apart from those days.

We have to be careful we don't hold onto things just because it's all we've known. Imagine if people got stuck in those 1950s tent meeting days. Sure, they were anointed for the time, but we can appreciate the fresh things of today. Take what you've learned from yesterday and incorporate it with the fresh things of God for today.

We also can't hold onto certain religious traditions just because we don't want God to impose a change in our lives. Some folks are content with dry religion because it allows them room to compromise. More than likely, the children of Israel listened to Balaam because he helped them feel comfortable with compromise under the guise of a religious practice. Religious tradition is a great promoter of compromise and can blind you from good discernment.

As we learn to sharpen our spiritual discernment, we need to realize that compromise will destroy it. Balaam, who I like to call the prophet of compromise, taught the people that certain lifestyles were OK all in the name of religion. Once they began to give ear to him, they let go of the principles they knew to be true. In other words, they lost their spiritual discernment and opened themselves to the wrong propaganda.

If there is any area of compromise in your heart today, chances are you know what that compromise is. The Lord is ready to forgive you, but the first step is to acknowledge its existence. That is often the hardest part, but if you learn the art of discerning your own life and wrong motives first and are willing to repent of them, you will be well on your way to becoming a strong and discerning believer!

Chapter Three

WARNING SIGNS OF A
SEDUCING SPIRIT

Now the Spirit speaketh expressly, that
in the latter times some shall depart from
the faith, giving heed to seducing spirits,
and doctrines of devils (1 Timothy 4:1).

Many years ago when we first started our church, we were recommended to meet a pastor by a long-time minister friend. He told us, "You need to meet these pastors; their anointing might be of interest to you because you like prophetic ministry." Most people who know us know that we like a certain dimension of the prophetic anointing.

Since all pastors need good ministerial friendships and we were looking for some who had a hunger for prophetic ministry, we decided to meet with them. Our friend told us where he was going to be preaching and that we should consider making the trip, so we went.

We got to the meeting, and the praise and worship style was a little different from anything we had experienced. It was very demonstrative and expressive. However, I have learned in my life that there are countless different expressions, music styles, and manifestations of the anointing for praise and worship. Therefore, I don't get too up in arms about worship services that are different from what I am used to. In other countries you see all sorts of demonstrative expressions in worship. I also know that different camps, circles, ministry networks, and even denominations can all have their flavor as well. There are many wonderful colors and styles in the Body of Christ, and I appreciate diversity when it is within biblical bounds.

Personally, I am not typically an advocate of excessive wildness just for the sake of being wild in praise and worship, but I do like some intensity and that overall sense of "high praise" filling the room. However, this church we attended with our friend took intense praise to a whole new level. People were wild, and I mean wild! They jumped around like popcorn for at least an hour! Of course, perhaps you are like me and you would rather have a little too much fire than none at all, so we found their worship to have a fresh dimension, even though it took us a minute to get used to it. Truthfully, they weren't really doing anything unbiblical.

As praise and worship came to a close, the pastor that our friend wanted us to meet called us out and prophesied to us. I mean, he could prophesy with power! Not only that, but his prophecy was very accurate regarding some things that had been on our hearts.

After the service, we all got together to meet the pastor and his wife and a few of their key leaders. The people were friendly and we really took a liking to their hunger for the prophetic. They seemed to have something uniquely zealous in their love for God.

The pastor carried a very bold, forthright ministry style, but that didn't bother us too much because many quality ministers also have a bold side to them. His preaching style was very revelatory and he was captivating to listen to. Sometimes he would say a few shocking things in the pulpit, but again, so do countless other pastors. So we thought, "It's probably fine."

After we got home, we decided to invite him to minister at our church, thinking maybe we just needed some fresh fire in our ministry. Our church was very new then and our worship team was in its very beginning years, so we agreed to allow them to bring their musicians. They came and ministered to our newly-formed, small congregation at that time. We had a church meeting with them that resembled some kind of prophetic explosion!

Most of it we really enjoyed, with just a few things that seemed of a different flavor. But the positive seemed to really outweigh anything negative, and at the time we chalked up many of these things to the fact that we perhaps needed to grow in some areas. I never want to miss something that is fresh from the Lord just because it isn't initially my "flavor."

What seemed to reassure our hearts that this ministry was OK was when this pastor told us that he was going to be hosting his annual conference and that the main speaker was a widely accepted and recognized prophet in the Body of Christ. We were familiar with that prophet's ministry, so we decided to go. We also took a number of our leaders and church members along on the trip. We were all hungry for a prophetic impartation from the Lord.

When we got to the meeting, we met several of the ministers and a couple other known prophets who were also speaking. One particular prophet (not the main speaker) called us out and, as expected, prophesied some very accurate things over us. He, too, had a fairly well-known ministry.

As time continued at the conference, we couldn't get away from the fact that there was just something that didn't seem right about these people. We just couldn't put our finger on what it was. We tried through the process of deduction but couldn't locate what it was that gave us a strange feeling. We kept reasoning to ourselves that one of the most widely recognized prophets was speaking there. They also had many prophetic characteristics and practices that are also widely accepted in the Charismatic, prophetic community. We also didn't think there was anything truthfully unbiblical about their new style of worship. It was just a little unusual sometimes. So what was it that we had reservations about?

We were invited the following day to breakfast by the pastor and the prophet who prophesied to us at the meeting. The other prophet who was the main speaker wasn't there, just these two. They began to talk to us about the fresh anointing and all seemed fine, but then the conversation turned to something different. They began to discuss how they had been coming into new revelation as of late. They started talking on the subject of eternal judgment and the devil. Then finally out it came—one of them said, "We don't believe there is a literal hell." They must have seen our shocked and reserved faces, because then they said, "Sure, we had a hard time with it in the beginning too, but now we see the truth, and we want to explain it to you."

That was it! That was the thing we couldn't put our finger on all that time. Now, while I don't think the pastor always believed this doctrine, at this point you could tell he was hooked. With that we quickly finished up breakfast and let them know we just couldn't agree with their views. Afterwards, we immediately headed out of town and cut all communication with them from that moment forward.

Later, we discovered that the one prophet we had breakfast with had strongly embraced this false doctrine prior to the conference we attended. Additionally, He was well acquainted with and preached for another pastor who at one time had one of the most influential churches in the Body of Christ. Undoubtedly the two had a common bond on the issue of there being no "literal" hell, because that influential pastor also fully embraced it and eventually lost his entire church and was labeled a heretic.

That same "prophet" also deeply influenced the pastor we were getting to know. Many years after we abruptly broke acquaintance with them, we found out that their church also fully embraced the same doctrine. We also learned that through that same "prophet's" influence, the church went from being a mainline Charismatic church into a form of orthodoxy that also didn't believe there was a literal hell. In addition, there were countless other blatant doctrinal things that they embraced until they got into gross error.

Here is the most alarming part: the "prophet" responsible for promoting much of this later began dressing in a unique version of priestly black garb and taking on an odd, almost fiendish appearance. I have noticed this tendency among people who embrace blatant false doctrine. Then, nearly a decade later, we found evidence that he was parading with a scantily clad woman and purposely promoting other compromising behavior in an effort to be "fresh and relevant."

As for the well-known prophet I mentioned who was to be the main speaker in the conference we attended, he didn't keep any connection to them either. Our friend that originally introduced us to this group of people also broke all ties with them. He was saddened that a ministry that had such great anointing and potential got so far off base. He felt bad for ever introducing us to them.

Commonly, we know this false teaching I have been referring to as a form of the *Doctrine of Universalism*, which has the premise that all beings will be reconciled to God. Therefore, the doctrine deducts that there can be no "literal" hell or eternal judgment as we typically understand it. Of course, there are many varying views on this doctrine, but this is the common idea.

While we will teach on how to correctly discern doctrine in another chapter, here I want to use the story of our experience to teach how the devil seduces people with evil spirits in order to get them offtrack in their walk with God and in their doctrinal beliefs. I have known so many believers who started out on the right path but unknowingly got involved with a seducing demon. We need to know the clear warning signs so we can discern the presence of seducing demons.

SEDUCING DEMONS

To get a clear picture, let's look first at this key and revelatory verse from Scripture.

> *Now the Spirit speaketh expressly, that in the latter times some shall depart from the faith, giving heed to seducing spirits, and doctrines of devils* (1 Timothy 4:1).

The verse starts with the phrase, *"the Spirit speaketh expressly."* This means that the Holy Spirit is giving us a strong and clear warning. His message isn't something we should just skim over or think will never apply to us. There are many verses of Scripture, but rarely do you find them written in this strong, cautionary tone.

What does the Holy Spirit want us to see? He begins with a reminder about the times. In Chapter One, I talked about how staying cognizant of the times will help keep you on the cutting edge of discernment. These seducing spirits or demons will be on the increase in the latter days, and we need to be more alert.

A seducing demon is not just sexual in nature. Many people associate the word "seduce" or "seduction" with being seduced sexually. It can be included in it, but that isn't the entire meaning of the word, nor is it the meaning in this verse.

The Greek word here is *planos*. It is also often translated in the New Testament as "deceiver." Very simply it means to rove as a tramp, an imposter, or misleader.[1]

Now, the key characteristic of these seducing demons is that they rove about—like homeless gypsies, literally! Think of what gypsies do. They go from place to place selling various novelties and magical cures, and they are always looking for a new prospect. They typically pretend to have special powers but often are looking for someone to trick just so they can make money. Gypsies never stay in the same place. They are discontent and always need a new environment, person, or place to fuel them. If they stay in one place too long, people might wise up to their deceptive behavior.

Think about the devil for a moment. The Bible says, *"Be self-controlled and alert. Your enemy the devil prowls around like a roaring lion looking for someone to devour"* (1 Pet. 5:8 NIV). He is always on the hunt, and he is never satisfied with his last kill. This is exactly how seducing spirits and demons operate. They move about like homeless wanderers, always looking for something or someone new to deceive.

The worst part is that they dress up like something they are not. They wear special "clothing" like gypsies do. In fact, some of these seducing demons will dress up and look like Christians! They might look like a best friend, business partner, or even a relative. Seducing spirits typically operate through people who have already been deceived into listening to them. However, they don't always have to appear in the form of a live person, but in the things people produce. They can dress up in the form of a favorite song, activity, pastime, or television program.

The key to remember is they wander around pretending to be something they are not.

THREE WARNING SIGNS OF SEDUCING DEMONS

Now, if we can remember that there are three main tricks seducing demons use, they become easier to recognize. From First Timothy 4:1 and from the meaning of the word "seducing" that we just studied, we see the deceptive warning signs of these demons. Seducing demons will try to make you:

1. Feel dissatisfied,

2. Depart from the faith, and

3. Want something they have to offer.

In a nutshell, you will always see these three signs with seducing demons. Let's talk about each of them in detail so you can understand what I mean.

SEDUCING DEMONS MAKE YOU FEEL DISSATISFIED

That is where the wandering comes from. When you're dissatisfied, you roam about, discontented, looking for something else. As we just read, the main characteristic of a seducing spirit is that they roam because they are always dissatisfied.

Here, the example of adultery provides a clear picture of this truth. Usually adultery in a marriage begins because one person (or both) becomes dissatisfied with their marriage. They stop feeling content with their spouse's personality, looks, and attitude, or they are just unhappy with their life. Perhaps they have spent too much time reading romance stories and watching movies that paint the perfect love relationship, or they've become discontent through exposure to sexually explicit material. In some cases, the dissatisfaction arises from previous sexual experiences or abuses that have never been properly dealt with.

The seduction to be unfaithful in the marriage relationship begins with a feeling of dissatisfaction that starts to tell a person, "There must be something better out there." If they give ear to that internal feeling or voice long enough, they will eventually act on their feelings.

That is just the obvious example we most often use. However, let's bring this same scenario over into church and Christianity. Many Christians live dissatisfied in some way.

For the more marginal and carnally-minded Christian, it will often come in material form. They find themselves unsatisfied with their occupation. In fact, many such people cannot find a consistent career path. They *roam* from job to job. They live through constant financial highs and lows. One minute they have money, and the next minute they are broke. They will go anywhere, move anywhere, or do whatever it takes to get that next feeling of satisfaction, but before long they are back to square one, as dissatisfied as they were at the last address, last job, and last relationship.

Some of these same people will move from house to house every few months or years. Have you ever noticed that pattern in people who come from a lifestyle of poverty? They hardly ever stay long at the same address, they never keep the same phone number, and they hardly ever have the same car. Many Christians, even from a more middle-class lifestyle, are not too different. They always want something different from what they have. They spend so much thought and energy striving for it that they rarely have time for the Kingdom of God. This is a seducing demon!

Some will say, "Yes, but isn't it OK to want to get ahead?" Sure, nothing is wrong with efforts for making a better living. It gets out of balance when you let dissatisfaction drive you. You look around at your car and wonder why the neighbors have a better one when they don't even serve God. Or you just can't feel happy on any one job because it doesn't feel at the moment like your getting a real financial payout from it. Some people are driven by the fact that they always wished they lived somewhere else. Really, it's just a form of covetousness—always wanting something different from what you have. Many people are deep in financial debt because dissatisfaction has driven them to buy things they could have done without.

First Timothy says, *"But godliness with contentment is great gain"* (1 Tim. 6:6). When you feel dissatisfied with your present situation, the best way to counteract that demon is to start looking at all the good things you presently have. Then let God increase and prosper you for the right reasons and through the right methods because you were, godly, consistent, and content. Then over time, your hardworking ethic pays off.

For the more spiritually focused Christian, dissatisfaction can work another way. There can be such a thing that many have referred to as a "holy dissatisfaction." By that I mean that we are not content to have mediocrity with God and we aren't happy with status quo, half-hearted American Christianity. We aren't content with dead, dry religion; we want the fresh manifestations of God.

That is how my husband and I have always felt. We want the "now" things of the Spirit. In our case, seducing spirits attempted to use that hunger or dissatisfaction to get us connected to people who were in error. We were spiritually dissatisfied and we wanted a fresh experience with God. The motive of our heart was right, but our method got off-track.

Many dedicated, Spirit-filled Christians get a similar feeling of spiritual dissatisfaction, and before you know it they go from church to church and can't ever get plugged in. They travel the nations finding the next big conference to tickle their fancy, but they end up right back in the same place looking for whatever is next. Eventually, if they aren't careful this habit connects them to the wrong things.

Some just live for the latest "revelation." Again, nothing wrong with wanting fresh revelation, but some are consumed with finding the latest insight and ultimately end up digging things out of the Bible inaccurately. This is where many preachers have gotten into trouble. In order to keep their ministry interesting to people, they want to come out with the latest "bang" in their preaching. They need the next big book title and spiritual "thriller," so to speak. In that quest, some preachers have gotten off-base in their revelation. This becomes a dissatisfaction fed by a seducing spirit.

I also know people who aren't in ministry that make this same mistake. Their spiritual dissatisfaction drives them to find some new, "never known before" depth in God. Of course, usually they ignore all the correct biblical principles they have had in front of them for years that will get them there. No, instead they need something new. They want a new spiritual "high." Some just want to come up with more knowledge than the pastor or the rest of the church people. They prance around like they know more than everyone else, and they sit through the pastor's sermon marking up their Bible with facial expressions of disagreement. Others will piously nod their head in agreement as if to say, "I already knew that!" Yet, some of those same people won't do the most basic things needed to be a true Christian.

They may also get on Internet blogs to show their great knowledge and often spend plenty of time slandering all the preachers who, in their perception, are ignorant. Of course, we will talk later about how to use correct discernment regarding pastors and preachers. However, here I want to focus on the fact that some people just want to be the most correct and knowledgeable, and in that effort they end up listening to a demon.

Is there anything wrong with wanting to experience new depths of revelation? Not at all, but it has to be for personal growth toward

God, not to prove yourself against others. So how do we avoid getting deceived in our quest to go deeper?

Keep this focus—*make the Lord your object of fulfillment, not your dissatisfaction.* When your goal is to pursue the Lord, God will automatically bring you to all that is needed to satisfy your life. Allow the Holy Spirit to divinely bring you the right people, situations, and revelations as you focus on Him. Let it happen naturally through consistent study, prayer, and church attendance. Don't go hunting for the latest and greatest Christian "outpouring" just because you need a fix and have decided nothing in your daily surroundings ever feeds you. Go to a conference because you want to set aside a few dedicated days for the Lord away from your normal routine or just to make a refreshing vacation out of it.

In the same way, get revelation because you are a consistent studier of the Bible and you really want to know God in a personal way. Ask yourself how this revelation is helping *you* become a person of better character. Don't study because you want to disprove all the teachings you dislike or be the next famous revelator of Scripture.

Let's be reminded of this verse in Ephesians: *"That we henceforth be no more children, tossed to and fro, and carried about with every wind of doctrine..."* (Eph. 4:14). Remember what seducing demons are. They are wanderers. They rove about from thing to thing. When we allow ourselves to become dissatisfied, we take on those same characteristics. We are tossed to and fro, but never really experience a heart change, never get ahead in life, and never become a true blessing to the Body of Christ.

Watch for signs of constant dissatisfaction and wandering. If you actually are dissatisfied in your church for a valid reason, then wait for the Lord until He leads you to the *right* church. Resist the temptation to become a church-hopper or uncommitted to church in general. Contentment and satisfaction in the Lord will keep you from seducing demons.

SEDUCING DEMONS ENTICE YOU TO
DEPART FROM YOUR FAITH

The second warning sign of a seducing demon is a drop in your faith levels or your personal Christian commitment. Usually, this begins through a lack of prayer and Bible reading.

Remember again our verse in First Timothy 4:1. It says, *"...some shall depart from the faith, giving heed to seducing spirits...."*

In all our years of ministry, I have never once known anyone who gave in to a seducing spirit without departing from the faith. They simply quit doing what they already knew and had learned to do over the course of many years. They quit praying as much as they used to. They watched more television than read the Bible. They tended to complain a lot. They spent more time at the mall or too much time talking on the phone. Seducing spirits love to lure you away from a life of daily consistency with spiritual things.

There are two main ways they get you to depart from the faith. To help us understand this, I have categorized faith into two definitions for clarity. They are:

- *Active faith*—This is the faith you use in prayer for getting your prayers answered and receiving miracles from God.

- *Committed faith*—This is the faith that forms your overall Christian commitment and foundational beliefs.

To begin, I can think of one specific story about how seducing demons like to pull people away from *active faith*. We had one particular service in our church on a Sunday night when the Holy Spirit moved in a unique way. God swept through the place, and people were laughing, crying, and falling under the Spirit's power. There was no preaching that night, just a move of the Holy Spirit.

During the service, we were praying for people to receive several types of miracle breakthroughs. One of them was in regards to rents and mortgages. During the recent time of recession in the United States, we knew many people who were in difficult situations in these areas. Now, we could all feel God touch these people. God spoke many things to this group of people about how some would get different homes but they would still be a blessing, others would get a miracle with the bank, and so on. But for everyone, the Lord concluded with this prophetic encouragement: "Don't worry; just let God take care of it."

However, over the course of the next few days following that Sunday, I overheard different people who had received prayer talking about how bad their housing situation was. I remember thinking to myself, "But don't they remember Sunday?" You see, instead of staying with what they had received in faith, they were fussing with the problem. Seducing spirits were working to get them to depart from the kind of active faith that expected a miracle.

From that, one person even toyed with the idea of moving out of state, hoping for a better day. When considering it, they didn't even pause to realize that in a new location they still would have to find a house and would also have to find work. They were just going because they were discouraged in their faith and had now become dissatisfied. They just saw the grass greener someplace else. They had no job offers or housing arrangements in the new city, but here they were employed. Their credit situation, housing situation, and job situation would not have changed by moving. But seducing spirits will blind your good senses and talk you into things when you allow yourself to depart from your faith!

Look at this verse of Scripture. *"Holding faith, and a good conscience; which some having put away concerning faith have made shipwreck"* (1 Tim. 1:19). Seducing demons want you to quit believing for your answer to prayer and start complaining so you will ultimately make decisions you will one day regret.

The devil also seduces you in your faith through attacking your *committed faith.* This is where he talks you into trading your long-trusted, stable beliefs, godly lifestyle, and tested doctrines for something new.

In my earlier story about the prophet we met, the devil wanted us to quit staying close to the long-trusted doctrines that we had not only learned in our Bibles but from trusted and godly pastors. Again, we never even once considered it, but I know it was the devil's plan. We thwarted that seducing demon by not departing from our faith!

Now I want to clarify a key point along these lines. This isn't to say that everything you have learned in the past was always an accurate doctrine. As I said, we will cover in detail how to correctly discern doctrine in a future chapter. However, here I want to make one key point. You can explore different doctrines and teachings that you are unfamiliar with *if* you keep three principles in operation.

1. Don't study them motivated out of frustration and dissatisfaction with some other doctrine or group of people. Otherwise you leave yourself vulnerable to demonic influence.

2. Stay connected to trusted, long-proven pastors and spiritual fathers and mothers and study the things they have taught you. Have people you can trust to give you an honest opinion on what you are receiving.

3. Look for churches, ministries and groups who are stable with credible and accountable ministries who have embraced the doctrines you

are looking into. It makes it much easier to trust what you are receiving when worldwide and sound ministries are also operating in what you are studying.

Keeping these in mind will help you study doctrine correctly. Since we've talked extensively on the first one already, let's focus here on the second principle and we will touch on the third principle in several places throughout this book. For now, relating to the second principle above, Paul told Timothy, *"But continue thou in the things which thou hast learned and hast been assured of, knowing of whom thou hast learned them"* (2 Tim. 3:14). Notice he told Timothy to continue in what he had already learned from trusted, proven sources. Listen to your pastor and leaders who have stood the test of time.

Of course, this doesn't mean that there isn't revelation beyond what you have already known or what you've always heard. It means spending time solidifying what you *have* learned before you go looking for something else.

A good example is with tithing. Some people don't like to tithe. They don't want to give up that extra money every month. Because of this, they probably never studied about tithing out of an attempt to avoid it in their mind. Then they hear a guy on the radio teach that tithing is not a New Testament practice. Suddenly their chord of dissatisfaction has been struck and they now have a new interest in studying the subject. They think, "Wow! I always knew there was another side to that tithing doctrine!" Problem is, they never studied the first side. Their first attempt at studying the subject was to disprove it.

Instead, they should have listened to the teaching of countless trusted and proven pastors and studied that. Now it comes with an attempt to prove it wrong.

This is a practice of many Christians when it comes to Bible study and exploring doctrine. Of course, many will immediately say here, "Yes, but when I did study, I still found clear evidence that the original view was wrong!" There probably are those cases. However, there is a danger with this habitual approach to study, because it comes with the *deliberate* intent to depart from some teaching or long-proven ministry you didn't like. Then, even if the doctrine was true, you've already formed a mindset that it is false. The reason you are working to prove it wrong in the first place is because you have already decided not to agree with it, right or wrong.

See how the Bereans in the Book of Acts studied doctrine. With readiness of mind, they received the Word that was preached to them through proven sources (see Acts 17:11). That means they listened, they were ready to receive it, and *then* they further studied to become assured of these doctrines in their own hearts.

Now, keep in mind I am talking about a positive study of long-time trusted doctrines that represent our committed faith. I am *not* referring to receptive study of the new, the peculiar, and that which is only accepted by a small few as indicated in the third principle above. This is in keeping with the Scripture we just read when Paul was speaking to Timothy. He said, *"continue thou in the things which thou hast learned and hast been assured of..."* (2 Tim. 3:14). He is saying to first continue in the things you have *already* learned. That means you take what your pastors, mentors, and trusted ministers are teaching on a wide scale, and you study them. You get them down into your heart and know what the Bible says until you become, as the verse says, *"assured of"* them. The word "assured" means to find trustworthy.

I believe it is wise to first study the widely accepted view, especially when the wider view is what is acceptable in most circles. While we can't always go with the masses, there is a reason certain beliefs have stayed with the Church for years.

Again, Paul told Timothy, *"...knowing of whom thou hast learned them"* (2 Tim. 3:14). He is saying that there is safety in staying close to the sources that have a long track record of stable ministry and proven fruit. There is usually a good reason their ministry has not only lasted but has been fruitful for many years. In the same passage, Paul also said, *"Now you have closely observed and diligently followed my teaching, conduct, purpose in life, faith, patience, love, steadfastness..."* (2 Tim. 3:10 AMP). Stay close to the long-trusted, proven ministries with stable fruit. Doing so will help you to not depart from your faith.

SEDUCING DEMONS OFFER TO FULFILL WANTS OR NEEDS

The third main warning sign of a seducing demon is they present things that we often need or simply desire. These things come in a package that is familiar and tailor-made for us. Demons watch our lives. They take note of our personal experiences from the time we are born. They notice what you talk about and what television shows interest you, and they watch the level of your spiritual lifestyle. They know what your weak areas are and what things get you excited. Seducing demons will talk to you in a way you will receive. They will identify with something in your life and speak to that area, making you feel as if a longtime need or desire is finally being met.

This is why so many Christian people confuse a seducing spirit with the Holy Spirit. The Holy Spirit wants our needs met, so demons will pretend to bring you answers but through the wrong methods. They come promising emotional stability, healing from the pain of abuse, personal fulfillment, happy relationships, job promotion, ministerial success, physical healing, and more. These seem wonderful because they are all the things God wants us to have, but demons will bring them through means that are opposed to Scripture and not from God.

Seducing spirits always have something you want or something that relates to you personally. Often it's something that makes you feel good about yourself or finally vindicated in some fashion.

I have heard of and read books—fiction books and also teaching books—that have subtle, borderline-false, or wrong doctrines in them. Yet because the story or narrative relates to the personal challenges and struggles of people's lives, they fall in love with the material and think it's from God. Often, regardless of the doctrine, if the content relates enough to the hurt inside people they usually won't discern the false doctrine or wrong teaching in it. When that happens, people often adjust their views on the subject to match the book or article they read. In fact, sadly this is how many Christians get their spiritual input, because they don't spend time delving into their Bibles as much as they do other things.

In my story at the beginning of this chapter, we identified with the prophetic dimension of the ministry we were introduced to. It spoke to our personal interests and spiritual hunger. In other words, we could relate to their anointing, and they made us feel like we had friends who were on the same page.

My husband and I have always had a heart for the ministry. It's all we ever wanted to do in our lives. Years ago, just before we started our church, we were presented with an opportunity to pastor a church in another state. It was a larger church that had a school campus, radio program, and all sorts of other ministries. You could wonder what young pastor wouldn't want a ministry like that. However, God had been speaking to us about starting a church. We had received countless prophecies, pastoral confirmation, and other input until we knew we were supposed to go to Omaha and start a church. However, if you were to reason it all out in your mind you could find yourself saying, "Why start a church from scratch? This one already has everything a pastor could want."

We turned down the offer for this other church because we just felt we would have missed God. Thank God we did, because we found out later that the church had been filled with division, strife, and countless other terrible problems. Had we gone there just because we wanted a big ministry, we would have walked into a potential disaster.

However, I know many pastors and ministers who get caught up this way. A seducing demon, feeding their pride or even their sincere desire to do something for God, talks them into all sorts of compromises, inconsiderate behavior, or in some cases terrible sins. Again, the demons presented something these pastors wanted.

Look again at Ephesians:

> *Then we will no longer be immature like children. We won't be tossed and blown about by every wind of new teaching. We will not be influenced when people try to trick us with lies so clever they sound like the truth* (Ephesians 4:14 NLT).

Seducing demons have clever ways of speaking lies in a way that sounds like the truth. Look at this verse also in Second Timothy talking about how people are used by seducing spirits and how they deceive:

> *They will act religious, but they will reject the power that could make them godly. Stay away from people like that! They are the kind who work their way into people's homes and win the confidence of vulnerable women who are burdened with the guilt of sin and controlled by various desires* (2 Timothy 3:5-6 NLT).

What do they do? They relate to a person's personal challenges, failures, needs, and desires. This verse mentions women here because they tend to get deceived by emotions more than men typically do. However, many men follow deceptive feelings and personal desires, so this verse should be a warning for both men and women. The emotions connected to struggles and certain experiences govern some people so heavily that they are extremely vulnerable to seducing spirits.

These verses say that these spirits win your confidence. They come offering a sense of rescue and the kind of answers that you are open to hear in light of your situation. That is how seducing demons seduce! They have something tailor-made for you personally, and it feels like the solution you've always been waiting for.

This is why we have to be students of the Bible and study the doctrines and truths that form our walk with God. We must hold ourselves accountable to the biblical method, whether or not it makes us feel better at the moment. It was our strong foundation in the Scriptures that made us uneasy when that pastor and prophet tried to teach us some other doctrine. It gave us the ability to discern the truth in spite of all the other good experiences we had with these people. Had we stayed connected to them because of our desire to have friends in the prophetic ministry, we probably would have gotten into error and ruined our future.

Don't allow unhealthy dissatisfactions, a departure from your faith, or an excessive focus on getting personal needs met to become the things that form your views or decisions. Let those things come from the Word of God, prayer, the stability of a good church, and a content Christian lifestyle. It will keep your defenses raised against the deceptive nature of seducing spirits!

ENDNOTE

1. King James Version Greek Lexicon, "Planos," Online Bible Study Tools, Definition, http://www.biblestudytools.com/lexicons/greek/kjv/planos.html (accessed July 8, 2010).

Chapter Four

DEVELOPING SKILLS FOR EXCELLENT DISCERNMENT

...Those who by reason of use have
their senses exercised to discern both
good and evil (Hebrews 5:14).

The entire purpose of having spiritual discernment is so we can tell the difference between good and evil. The fact that the Bible tells us that we need discernment is our indicator that it may not always be easy to tell the difference. A lack of discernment combined with demons masquerading as angels of light causes many people to become confused (see 2 Cor. 11:14).

Biblical discernment is a necessary tool available to *every* believer. It isn't a special gift or ministry calling. The Bible gives us no evidence of such a "calling" as some have claimed to be specially called to. Whenever the Scripture speaks of spiritual discernment, it does so in light of our Christian walk and it applies to every Christian.

This is entirely different from the *gift of discerning of spirits* as mentioned in First Corinthians, which lists the nine gifts of the Holy Spirit (see 1 Cor. 12:10). This gift is a momentary supernatural occurrence from the Holy Spirit, just as are all the other spiritual gifts listed there. It isn't a lifelong calling. Of course, depending on your ministry it could perhaps manifest often in your life, just as prophecy or a word of knowledge may operate often for a prophet. Discerning of spirits typically manifests supernaturally as a vision, spiritual experience, dream, or quick thought. It gives you the ability to see into the realm of the spirit so you can easily differentiate the types of spirits, good or bad, that are at work in a situation. It is a supernatural way of differentiating between good and evil.

Christian discernment, on the other hand, is different from that. It is a developed skill that comes from practice, just as you develop skill in using a bow and arrow or similar tool. *Every* believer should practice their skills for good discernment, and that is the purpose of this chapter. Being a discerning Christian is something you make a part of your spiritual foundation.

The need for discernment is obvious today, as good Christian people have become so confused in differing right from wrong that they are literally calling evil things good and good things evil. For example, they can watch the latest dance competition on television with dancers making seductive moves and wearing revealing costumes. They'll watch it several nights in a row just so they can find out the winner, but in turn will criticize people who jump, dance joyfully, and lift their hands in church to the Lord. They will discern the "wrong" in the church far more quickly than the actual wrong that is in the world, as many support the efforts of Hollywood more than they defend the Bible. Some Christian people are so dull in their discernment that they couldn't recognize evil and demons if they bit them in the nose!

The other concern we often run into is the dilemma of how to have strong discernment without becoming overly critical of everybody and everything. Some have so overemphasized the need for discernment that it has created paranoia. I have heard some go so far to say that children shouldn't even own a stuffed animal because it represents some form of idolatry and that demons can hide inside their stuffing! Sure, demons can hide in objects, and I do believe in that. However, we can also over-act in our efforts to be discerning until we become extremists with a religious spirit.

Others who claim to be discerning are just plain disagreeable and critical. They believe they are somehow specially gifted with this ability. They have made themselves the voice of discernment in the church when really it's just a critical spirit that finds self-confidence in always pointing the finger.

These differing scenarios show the need for us to lay out some basic principles in discernment, and if we put them into practice, we can learn to discern things biblically and correctly.

SHARPEN YOUR EDGE

I love to cook, so a few years ago I decided it was time for me to invest in a quality set of cooking knives. I felt so amazed when I got home to use them. They cut through all the food so precisely, and I was thrilled. I carefully read all the instructions on care and cleaning of my knives. I quickly learned that one of the key requirements in the use of quality kitchen knives is that they need regular sharpening. The manual encouraged sharpening prior to each use or two. That is because with *every* use the perfect alignment of the edge is slightly compromised and needs to be realigned in order to stay sharp. It is also true that cooking with a dull knife is actually more dangerous than using one that is razor sharp. The reason is that a dull knife puts you at risk for errors. With a dull knife, you have a great deal more resistance and you can slip and seriously hurt yourself.

Another thing I discovered about good kitchen knives is there is a skill to using them correctly. With the correct slicing or chopping techniques, you can actually be more efficient in the kitchen.

I have learned that good spiritual discernment is a lot like my kitchen knives. Our discernment needs two things:

1. Regular sharpening

2. Proper technique

Too many people who want sharp spiritual discernment do neither. That is why they ultimately find themselves making poor judgment calls even though they are filled with the Holy Spirit.

Let's begin with regularly sharpening our discernment. We will discuss proper techniques for discernment later in the chapter.

If you can imagine yourself like a sharp knife in the spirit, you can quickly see that every day your razor-sharp edge is up against some serious resistance. From the time you head out to work in the morning to face the world, the devil is going to try to attempt to pull you down spiritually. Some attempts are very subtle and hard to detect. It could be the talk radio program on the way to work discussing middle-aged people's risks of a specific health problem. If you are middle aged, you could immediately try to think of any symptoms you may have had relating to the health problem mentioned. If there are some similarities, you could easily get into fear and worry and start thinking of all kinds of potential outcomes.

Your edge has now been dulled slightly, the same way a knife is when it cuts a tomato. Sure, the knife doesn't lose all its sharpness in one use, nor does cutting a tomato or two put its effectiveness out of commission. However, the edge, while undetectable at that point, has lost a degree of the perfect alignment that makes it razor sharp. The more that knife is used against some resisting surface without sharpening, the more it will become dull.

In the same way, dealing with life's daily issues in a spiritually hostile and worldly environment may not wear down your spiritual discernment all at once. But over time, unless you sharpen it again your discernment will become dull.

This is where we so often make our biggest mistake. We assume, because we are strong, dedicated Christians who serve in church, pray with the intercessors, and even prophesy, that we are automatically sharp in our discernment. What we don't realize is that our edge might be getting dull because it has been encountering some resistance.

We can get some further insight into this from Hebrews, which says:

> *For every one that useth milk is unskilful in the word of righteousness: for he is a babe. But strong meat belongeth to them that are of full age, even those who by reason of use have their senses exercised to discern both good and evil* (Hebrews 5:13-14).

Notice it says *"have their senses exercised." Senses* here means perception, while the word *exercised* means "to train or practice." In modern terms, you could paraphrase verse 14 this way: *"Strong meat is for the mature, and those who feed on meat regularly are training their perception to judge the difference between good and evil."*

Now, my kitchen knife set came with a sharpening tool known as a "steel." It's a stainless steel tool, and when you run the edge of the knife against it a certain way the blade, also made of steel, gets realigned.

When you feed on the strong meat of God's Word every day—referred to in Scripture as a sharp sword—you are realigning your edge of discernment (see Eph. 6:17). Each time you open your Bible, you are taking the spiritual "steel" of that Scripture and using it to realign your edge. While you may not realize it at the moment, you are training yourself in discernment. God's Word used regularly trains your perceptivity to operate correctly. Then, each time you go out into the world in a spiritually hostile place, your discernment is up for the task.

I am amazed at how a soft, *powerless* tomato can dull a razor-sharp, *powerful* knife. Seemingly, a tomato is no match for a knife! A knife can turn a tomato into tomato puree in no time! But if you place that knife up against a truck load of tomatoes and never sharpen the knife in between, eventually the tomatoes will win. The only thing that can realign that knife is a steel that is more powerful than the knife itself.

We as believers are powerful in the spirit. Just like a knife over a tomato, we can defeat the devil and overcome the world in no time. Satan is no match for what we carry and he knows it, so he uses the art of distraction. He keeps us busy and distracted with barely enough time for a break. Satan is doing everything he can to keep us away from the sharpening steel. He knows that if you will pause long enough to get back in the training ring with your Bible, then he is no match against you. Your razor-sharp discernment will cut him off every time! That is because, no matter what situation he tries to use to wear your discernment down, you keep sharpening it again and again against something more powerful than yourself—the Word of God. God's Word is the steel that has more power than you do, and it is the first and most important thing toward realigning your perception.

Another way you sharpen your discernment is through other Christians. You have probably read this verse: *"Iron sharpeneth iron; so a man sharpeneth the countenance of his friend"* (Prov. 27:17).

Again, it's another "steel" that will help you realign your blade in the spirit. However, remember that for a steel to be effective it has to be of equal or greater power or strength. We established that the Word of God has that unchanging quality. However, not every person who calls themselves a Christian does. To sharpen your discernment with other believers, you need Christian fellowship or interaction from people whose lives and actions continually admonish you to walk in righteousness. They feed the fire in your spiritual walk and their lives push you to be a better Christian. This probably means you need people who are strong in God and perhaps aren't always willing to agree with you.

You can't just handpick two people in the world you like, invite them over for weekly prayer and coffee, and call it sufficient. You need a good church with a good pastor and full of strong Christians, so that every time you attend it is hard to be a loner or backslider! That is the true meaning of iron sharpening iron.

Lastly, another key way to sharpen your discernment is by praying in tongues. Often referred to in Scripture as praying in the Holy Ghost or praying in the spirit, there is something about it that gives you God's eyes into the spirit realm (see 1 Cor. 14:14-15). That is why it's referred to as praying *in the spirit*. It opens the spirit realm so you get God's perspective and can see what He sees. Praying in tongues makes you sensitive to the unseen realm around you, but it does so with the power of God guiding it. You're naturally more aware of the activity of demons and angels, but you also know what to do about them.

One example is Stephen. We find just as the protesters were ready to stone him, Stephen had an open vision of Heaven. However, the Bible makes a point to mention: *"But he, being full of the Holy Ghost, looked up steadfastly into heaven, and saw the glory of God..."* (Acts 7:55). There was a connection between the infilling of the Holy Spirit and his vision or the Bible wouldn't have mentioned them in context together.

We know from the Book of Acts that the main characteristic of the infilling of the Holy Spirit is speaking in tongues. I wouldn't be surprised if Stephen made a habit of praying in tongues and that was what caused him to see easily into the spirit. His perception that came through the power of the Holy Spirit also gave him the wisdom and ability to discern good from evil, and he chose the good by forgiving those who stoned him and being willing to die for the Lord (see Acts 7:60).

You are in the spirit when you pray in tongues. While you may not always see into the spirit with your physical eyes when praying in tongues, your perception becomes sensitive to that realm. You begin to take on more advanced revelation regarding the spiritual war surrounding you. It becomes so clear it makes discerning between good and evil easier.

Many Christians have become oblivious to the angelic and demonic activity in the heavens and as a result have dull discernment. They are often unaware that angels or demons are in the same room with them. They are also less sensitive to God who moves and operates in the realm of the spirit. We need revelation into the realm of the spirit if we are going to have accurate spiritual discernment. Praying in tongues acts like the door that connects your spirit to the realm of the spirit. With it we can pull the curtain back on the devil's schemes and better counter against him!

HUMAN PERCEPTION OR SPIRITUAL DISCERNMENT

The human spirit is just that—a spirit—and it has the ability to have insight into the spirit realm. We don't just possess this ability when we become born again and Spirit-filled. Yes, praying in tongues gives you God's insight and perspective into that realm; however, human spirits even without the Holy Spirit have a degree of sensitivity to the unseen realm. They just may not realize it.

Recently, I saw a television reenactment about a man who went to a tropical island for vacation and while swimming was attacked by a shark and lost one of his legs. He was a successful businessman, dedicated husband, and overall good person, but it was evident in the program he was not a dedicated, born-again Christian. So his spirit had not been reborn.

He had been swimming more than once with his wife on the beach at his hotel resort. On one particular morning he went out alone to swim. However, on this day he indicated that something felt different. For whatever reason, on the same beach that day the water seemed murky and something made him feel like he shouldn't go, but he just shrugged that feeling away and went into the water. That was when the shark attacked. There was apparently some perception in his spirit that something bad was going to happen. Notably, without the Holy Spirit he didn't possess the ability to understand it nor discern how to respond, but his spirit knew something was wrong.

Perhaps you have heard people relate similar stories. They might say things like they had a feeling not to take a certain route for work that day, but then did it anyhow. On the way they came upon an accident scene that made them extremely late to work and they found themselves saying, "Why didn't I go with my feelings and just go the other way?"

The human spirit is naturally perceptive to the realm of the spirit where there is no time or distance. That is why witches and spirit mediums can make contact with the spirit realm via their own spirit. When they do, however, because they *don't* have the Holy Spirit, they make contact with demons. On the other hand, we who are filled with the Holy Spirit connect with the Lord and get insight through the anointing. God not only enables us to see it, but also to discern how to respond in line with Him.

Human spirits can also be perceptive simply by taking in natural information that gives them a sense of things that might be happening in the spirit. For example, if you know someone who cannot seem to overcome an addiction, it is easy to "perceive" there is a demon of bondage working in their life.

We see this type of perception with the woman at the well when she *perceived* Jesus was a prophet (see John 4:19). She got that revelation because Jesus had just told her the personal secrets of her life. Her perception came from observation. The word *perceive* in John 4:19 is the Greek word *theoreo* which means "to perceive by watching or observing."[1] Initially, she knew Jesus was a prophet because she saw Him operate as one, but in turn her natural perception helped her receive the ultimate spiritual revelation Jesus wanted her to have.

The Spirit of God added divine revelation to her natural perception, because by the time her conversation with Jesus was over she was no longer calling Him just a prophet. Instead, she now began to indicate that she *perceived* Him to be the Messiah (see John 4:25,29). In verse 25 she says, *"I know that Messias cometh...."* The word "know" here is the word *eido* which means "to see, have a revelation or divine perception."[2] She went from natural perception that came by observation to a divine perception that came from revelation. Later she says, *"...is not this the Christ?"* (John 4:29).

Many Christians use the same kind of natural perception when they prophesy to people. They can deduct a lot about a person by how they carry themselves, how they dress, what they do for a living, or just the look on their face. They will often prophesy regarding things that relate to what they can see of the person outwardly. Just like the woman at the well, there is absolutely nothing wrong with this kind of perception, because it is often the starting block that fuels your perception in the spirit. Then the Holy Spirit uses it to bring supernatural revelation and inspiration.

In any case, the human spirit has in its creative makeup the capabilities for spiritual perception, but spiritual perception alone is different from spiritual discernment. The unsaved and witches can operate in perception. In short, *perception* is the ability to see into something or have an experience whether natural or supernatural, while *discernment* helps you know its source and how to respond in righteousness once you have seen it. Perception knows something is there, while discernment separates the good from the bad and gives you direction.

Many Christians have perception, but they never go the next step and learn to walk in discernment. Thus they become goofy with spiritual things, always out in la-la land, hearing and seeing strange things.

To learn the skills for good discernment, we have to know that perception and discernment will work together. At the same time, we don't want to mistake simple human perception with the spiritual discernment that comes from the Holy Spirit.

With that said, take one more glance at our Scripture: *"...have their senses exercised to discern both good and evil"* (Heb. 5:14). The word *senses* here is speaking of perception. In this case, it is the ability to perceive either by natural observation or divine revelation, but this word specifically relates to helping you understand the things of God. However, for simplicity we can just say "perception."

This verse is telling us that whatever type of perception we are operating in, it also needs to be trained in discernment. As I said, you can perceive things, Christian or not, but can you discern them correctly? The word *discern* in this verse means to judge or to draw an analytical conclusion. As Christians, we can't just stop at perception; we need the next part, and that is the ability from the Holy Spirit to analyze the information we receive and draw a godly conclusion. That is discernment.

THE CANDLE OF THE LORD

To recognize the voice of discernment, we need to understand where it speaks from. The human spirit is not only perceptive, it is the place where the Holy Spirit lives for the believer. That is why our capabilities in perception are so much more powerful than those of the non-Christian. We can see things from God and are able to discern them, separating the evil from the good. The world is at a disadvantage because they don't have the Lord inside teaching them what is good. That is why many people in the world today are busy defending criminal behavior, indecent clothing styles, and violent forms of entertainment and think it is normal and appropriate. They might perceive or see the evil on something, but they can't discern it. In other words, they can't rightly analyze it and draw any godly conclusions.

God lives on the inside of us, helping us draw the right conclusions about the information we take in. In other words, He is your voice of discernment, and He is speaking from inside your spirit. Look at Proverbs: *"The spirit of man is the candle of the Lord, searching all the inward parts of the belly"* (Prov. 20:27). This verse means that the candle or light of God speaks from within in you. His light and revelation will come deep from within, so deep that it causes you to examine yourself.

This is why I have trouble with people who can only discern the wrong in others but can't ever see or admit to any wrong in themselves. This verse reveals that when God's light begins speaking from your spirit, it will first search you out and cause you to come under God's examination.

God's voice will often sound like your own voice and conscience. Sometimes it will be a sensation or feeling about something. Learn to respond to those sensations. Your perception and in turn discernment may be trying to tell you something. If you have been doing the needed things to keep it sharp, it will be even clearer to you.

For example, if you hear a movie trailer come on the television, but right from the first second or two the music sounds creepy and something just feels strange, turn the channel quickly. Many people don't do that. They know they should turn the channel, but the remote is across the room or they are just curious as to what movie this is. So they ignore their perception that felt something strange and ignored discernment that told them not to put that before their eyes. God's voice of discernment down in your spirit will always push you away from worldly influences and toward righteousness.

TECHNIQUES FOR USING DISCERNMENT

As I mentioned with my new kitchen knives earlier, you need to keep them razor sharp, but if you don't want to get hurt it's equally important to use the proper cutting techniques.

I realized after getting better knives that my previous techniques were often wrong. In fact, I didn't realize I had been cutting things incorrectly in order to adjust to a dull knife. You know, things like sawing back and forth on a tomato skin or pushing down harder on a piece of meat because nothing seemed to be happening. It wasn't a pretty picture, never like the chefs on television! But after using my new knives, I realized that I couldn't cut things that way anymore.

In fact, until I learned better handling of these sharper knives, I caused myself a few injuries. But with some practice, I began to use a chef's knife better. Perhaps I am still no television chef, but good techniques have made food preparation much more efficient. I practiced how to better hold the knife in one hand and stabilize the food item in the other. I also practiced how to correctly move it across the cutting board.

In the same way, not only do we need sharp discernment, but we need to know how to handle it once we receive it. Some people are reckless with their discernment. For example, when they do discern something accurately, their response is extreme and excessive. They go overboard and do things like hurt people's feelings unnecessarily, make abnormal clothing choices, or just make life miserable for themselves and others.

I remember when I was a teenager going on a road trip with a church group to an athletic event. We travelled home late that night and restaurants were few and far between. Everyone was very hungry and we wanted to eat. We kept stopping at restaurants and all the kids would wait in the bus for a few minutes while one of the chaperones went in to check it out. They kept coming out shaking their heads and we would have to leave. We even stopped at some grocery stores to encounter the same thing. I finally inquired of someone why we couldn't go in to eat in any of these places. Someone replied, "They sell alcohol in those stores and restaurants, so we won't give them any business." It wasn't until many miles later that we happened upon a fast food place that was still open. While I can appreciate their efforts to stand up for righteousness, the approach was all wrong. I remembered wondering how they bought groceries if they couldn't buy from a store or gas station that sells alcohol or cigarettes. I wonder if their ideals are still the same today, since nearly all establishments sell these things. Their technique perhaps needed some tweaking so they didn't put undue demands on themselves or others, just like I was doing with my new kitchen knives. They were so sharp I was endangering myself and needed to change how I was using them.

Here are some key techniques for using your sharp discernment correctly:

1. True discernment always examines itself first.

2. Judge the fruit without vengeance.

3. Truth must be mixed with love.

4. Good discernment avoids unnecessary extremes.

EXAMINE SELF FIRST

This is a good way to determine if your discernment is true spiritual discernment or just personal criticism and a way to avoid addressing issues in your own life.

> *Brothers, if someone is caught in a sin, you who are spiritual should restore him gently. But watch yourself, or you also may be tempted* (Galatians 6:1 NIV).

If you perceive someone is doing wrong, a person of good discernment responds by first looking at how they can avoid making similar mistakes. Pray for the person involved in wrongdoing and ask God to check your heart. Few people are quick to discern themselves when they see others get offtrack.

In some cases, it isn't about sin in another person; it's the sinful temptations that come in other various ways. When we discern the evil in it, we don't always pause to examine if it is having an ongoing negative effect or if it is tempting us.

The key is whenever your discernment recognizes evil you need to put yourself in check so you stay away from sin. It's hard to fall into a critical spirit with people or get into sinful behaviors when we are quick to examine our own potential shortcomings the moment we discern something is wrong.

JUDGE FRUIT WITHOUT VENGEANCE

We all know the Scripture in Matthew 7:1 that says, *"Judge not, that ye be not judged."* A lot of people who don't want to be accountable to any rule or structure will rehearse this verse because they think no one should analyze their sinful behavior and actually call it sin. They don't realize, however, that Jesus also said in the same chapter,

"...by their fruits ye shall know them" (Matt. 7:20). This means you will know if a person is walking in good or bad by what they do and how they act.

The word *judge* in Matthew 7:1 is *krino*. It is similar to "discern" but slightly different. It means to "properly differentiate or distinguish the good from the bad," but then follow up with some kind of revengeful punishment.[3] This can be done in a positive way against demonic powers as we declare God's judgment against them because the word *krino* also means *to execute judgment upon*. It becomes wrong when we do this against people and condemn them when we haven't been given any form of position to discipline them. That is what the verse means when it says *"judge not."* In other words, don't condemn someone with personal vengeance or self appointed disciplinary measures because if you do that, someone may do the same thing to you one day.

It is OK to look at people's actions, behaviors, and habits and separate the good from the bad. Good biblical discernment looks at the fruit of people's lives and makes decisions about how much to be involved with them or how to respond. A good way to know if someone's fruit isn't healthy is that it will shows signs of *constantly* being rotten, not just because they made a one-time mistake. Fruit is determined by a person's overall character, and there will *always* be signs that reveal what kind of fruit is growing on the tree of their lives.

Many Christians don't use discernment in choosing their friends. They will make close friendships with certain Christians or even non-Christians with all the wrong fruit who have all sorts of rebellious sin habits, bad attitudes, and ethics.

For example, they will befriend a person who has been financially dishonest with countless people in the church, or they will find a common bond with someone who always seems to engage in borderline worldly activities. Others use no discernment in making friendships with people who always criticize the church while they themselves have carnal behaviors.

Examining people's fruit isn't wrong. Where it becomes wrong according to Matthew 7:1 is when it is followed up with vengeful behavior, backbiting, and resentment, and especially the attempt to bring them under some kind of harsh discipline that isn't yours to give. At that point it falls outside of biblical boundaries. We cannot be revengeful with people simply because we feel mistreated or better than them somehow. We can't go spreading gossip about them, trying to make them lose their job, or finding ways to get back at them because in our estimation they deserve it! We shouldn't be starting protest committees and internet blogs against fellow Christians, pastors, and churches in an effort to hold them accountable when we aren't given that position of authority. That is what the Bible means when it says "judge not." We can, on the other hand, take an honest look at the fruit of someone or something as it relates to deciding our own involvement with them.

TRUTH MIXED WITH LOVE

Sometimes exercising sharp discernment means we have to take a stand that may not always be popular or can even be painful. We need to stand up these days for our convictions, but there is a right way to go about it. Most of us know the verse which says, *"Instead, speaking the truth in love, we will in all things grow up into Him who is the Head, that is, Christ"* (Eph. 4:15 NIV). This shows us that our maturity is evident by how we show love when taking a stand is necessary. Notice it says *"speaking the truth."* The context of this Scripture is about Bible doctrine and indicates to us the need for staying aligned with the Bible on things. Not only should we stay with truth, but we also need to stay aligned with the Bible on how we treat people. We shouldn't have a motive to discredit anyone, even when they've done wrong.

For example, perhaps you are questioned at work by your boss about a fellow employee's work ethic or some other wrongful behavior. Don't respond with, "Boy, I am so glad you are finally doing something about so-and-so! I have had it up to here with their slimy ways! They really get everybody upset around here." Sure maybe they have done wrong, but state truth mixed with love.

If you do have to stand for truth knowing painful results can't be avoided, seek to become part of the healing process for those affected whenever it's possible. That can be done directly or sometimes indirectly.

Maybe your local church is in turmoil because the pastor fell into some terrible sin. Sure, as Christians we need to stand for the truth, expecting that the pastor will be held accountable. But keep in mind, the actual process of pastoral discipline is not the job of church members, but other pastors and the established leadership in charge. However, you *can* stand for the truth with those leaders by trusting their judgment that they will do the right thing and by supporting the process in humble prayer. You can also be indirectly part of the healing by avoiding the spread of unnecessary discussion about the situation with family and friends and by supporting the new pastor who comes in, whether he is temporary or permanent.

I always feel badly when I hear of so-called Christians doing hurtful things like setting abortion clinics on fire and harming people who work there. Sure, sharp discernment says we need to stand against the evil practice of abortion, but good techniques in discernment show us better ways to go about it. We can speak the truth in love by supporting positive pro-life groups, adoption programs, or through church-sponsored awareness, but love doesn't seek anyone's hurt, even when they are clearly wrong.

AVOID UNNECESSARY EXTREMES

People in the church struggle all the time in this area. You have one group who is still dressing their kids in Halloween costumes and calling it innocent fun, while another group is burning Christmas trees and making vows to never again celebrate the holiday with a single piece of evergreen. Then we have others who make stringent rules about things that the Bible doesn't put the same rules on when practiced with godly prudence. At the opposite extreme are those who have almost joined the loose ideals of the hippies and their "live and let live" mentality, and they hardly have any godly boundaries about anything.

This is one of the key characteristics found in false doctrine. They are prone to extremes, so it is good to avoid these excesses. Philippians says, *"Let your moderation be known unto all men. The Lord is at hand"* (Phil. 4:5). The word *moderation* in many translations is often translated as "gentle," but it means to approach things gently in a mild-mannered way. Strong's actually says "appropriate." We are to handle all things we encounter with a modest and appropriate response, not with extremes such as excessive confrontation or, on the other hand, total unresponsive complacency.

Fashion choices are a good example because there is so much controversy surrounding them. Some people think its fine to dress in black gothic styles and be a Christian, while others think women can only wear long dresses and veils without a stitch of makeup. But let's look at the facts.

There is something that simply looks dismal about people who choose to wear spiked hair with black lipstick and nail polish. Whether people want to admit it or not, it just looks dark. Yet nowhere does the Bible actually say you can't wear black lipstick. It is just that the appearance of it leans toward a look of evil and at the same time is applauded by many in the occult. Look at the facts.

On the other hand, when you look at a nicely-dressed woman wearing soft pink lipstick and a comfortably fitting pantsuit or jeans, you naturally think it acceptable. She doesn't have to go without makeup or wear a dress from the 1800s, but her appearance is naturally acceptable and decent. The Bible doesn't say it is OK for a woman to wear that kind of makeup or blue jeans either. But again, look at the factual characteristics.

In these more controversial matters we now have to rely on Scriptures that talk about what is modest and *appropriate* and what is best representative of the Kingdom of God. Simply said, what best imitates Jesus?

What should a good Christian woman choose—a low-cut blouse and short shorts, or a long sleeve dress that starts at the neck and ends at the ankles? In this case, neither should be our answer. Our answer should be something decent and *appropriate* that becomes a Christian. The same approach applies to men. Dress in a modest style that is in keeping with the times, but not crossing the line into looking like the loose appearance of the world.

We need a balanced, appropriate response to the things that the Bible doesn't place specifics upon. Of course, these are very different from the things the Bible is clear about such as lying, stealing, homosexuality, and fornication. But on the issues we have known for years to be more debatable in the church, we should personally determine them from a standpoint of what is representative and appropriate to the Kingdom of God. That is what it means to be moderate.

For example, I personally cannot support the festivities of Halloween because the entire premise of the holiday is about fear and evil, and you can't find a way to derive anything Christian from it. On the other hand, I see no harm in having a Christmas tree because I can make it a decoration that enhances the atmosphere of worship surrounding our Savior's birth and the lights give off a heavenly feeling. Additionally, I can find reasonable and biblical spiritual meanings in a tree, even if there is great debate among some Christians over its origin.

Still, I don't take excessive approaches to either, and I make sure not to live in extremes. I don't stomp around town putting down all the Christian ladies' groups who wear pumpkins on their sweatshirts in October, nor do I make it my life's mission to promote the great spiritual symbolisms behind St. Nicolas, candy canes, and boughs of holly. Good discernment techniques will avoid these unnecessary extremes.

If you personally can find God in something and it is devoid of evil, demonic, or blatant worldly characteristics and the Bible makes no undeniable stance against it, then take a modest approach in how you participate. Lean toward the side of prudence with it if you do think it acceptable.

On the other hand, if it contains dark, sinful, and worldly characteristics, then make a personal decision to avoid it while realizing not everyone, especially out in the non-Christian world, understands your position on it. React to them with a wise, gentle, and moderate approach.

If we continually do the things necessary to keep our discernment sharp and use the proper and wise techniques for handling it, we can become very valuable in the advancement of God's Kingdom. We need these kinds of discerning believers in the Church today! Make a point of practicing the principles for using good discernment and your edge will stay properly aligned with God. Your determination to do so will be a blessing and a safeguard not only in your own life but in the lives of countless others.

ENDNOTES

1. *Vine Expository Dictionary of New Testament Words,* Unabridged. "Perceive" "Theoreo," http://www2.mf.no/bibel/vines.html (accessed August 20, 2010).

2. SearchGodsWord.org, "Eido," Bible Study Resources from HeartLight.org, Definition, http://www.searchgodsword.org/lex/grk/view.cgi?number=1492 (accessed July 9, 2010).

3. SearchGodsWord.org, "Krino," Bible Study Resources from HeartLight.org, Definition, http://www.searchgodsword.org/lex/grk/view.cgi?number=2919 (accessed July 9, 2010).

Chapter Five

TESTING DOCTRINES OF DANGER

Study to shew thyself approved unto God, a
workman that needeth not to be ashamed, rightly
dividing the word of truth (2 Timothy 2:15).

Everyone was standing on their feet, shouting and applauding. The excitement in the room was high and I was standing there with everyone else, getting caught up in the euphoria of the moment. That was until I heard some things that began to alert me. *Hmmm,* I thought. *Did they really mean that?* I wondered if the preacher had just made a mistake in their Bible interpretation or perhaps didn't choose their words correctly. Maybe they were still developing their revelation of Scripture along these lines, and for the most part I wasn't initially concerned. I've made those same mistakes when trying to communicate a point, and I want to be understanding when it unintentionally happens to someone else. As the preaching continued, however, I found myself slowly sitting back in my chair as the crowd continued to shout. I decided I needed time to write down and process some of the information and didn't want to keep shouting amen to something I wasn't sure about. Of course, I also didn't want to appear in disagreement since I always like to be supportive.

In this situation, the preaching wasn't the part that really bothered me the most. What really bothered me was the crowd's response to it. Not once did they stop cheering, jumping, and shouting. They were so caught up in the atmosphere that I wondered what anyone could have said from the pulpit that night. From what I could tell, it didn't seem anyone was actually *hearing* what was being said, they were just following the thunderous vibrations of the room. People were just enjoying the experience and seemed less concerned about the actual information being presented. If they *were* actually hearing the preaching, then they were receiving some ideas that weren't biblical.

I share this story not to make us wary of preachers. Most are good and certainly aren't dangerously or intentionally leading people astray. My concern here was whether or not we as believers are considering what we are hearing and accepting as the "biblical" truth. Do we know our Bible so that when something *is* preached we can effectively test it against the Word of God? Or are we following wrong doctrines and teachings just because we liked the atmosphere or person that presented them?

Some get into wrong doctrines because they want something they feel is fresh from God but don't take time to check out what they are hearing. This can be a problem in some circles, especially in the charismatic churches because we always want the fresh moves of God. Some simply spend too little time in the Bible or they don't use the right guidelines for correctly interpreting Scripture. In other cases, people ignore the guidelines because they want preaching that sounds edgy and up-to-date. Therefore, their tendency is to gravitate toward just about any doctrine they feel goes against the traditional teaching they believe to represent "old-school" religion.

In this chapter, I want to provide some guidelines for correctly interpreting Scripture as well as outline some characteristics for recognizing wrong or false doctrine. It is important for every discerning Christian to know the difference between false doctrine and harmless teaching mistakes. There are people who label things as false when they aren't false at all and vice versa. By examining a few key characteristics, we can more readily separate them from each other.

DILIGENCE CREATES ACCURACY

To begin, let's take a quick refresher on a Scripture familiar to many. Second Timothy says, *"Study to shew thyself approved unto God, a workman that needeth not to be ashamed, rightly dividing the word of truth"* (2 Tim. 2:15). Of course, the verse begins with the word *study*. It means to put diligent effort into it. That is something few people like to do these days in our get-everything-in-a-flash, "microwave" society! We don't want to put long hours into much of anything. But if we are going to handle the Word of God correctly and be alert to wrong doctrine, we simply can't take shortcuts. We have to become students of our Bibles so we won't fall or *"be ashamed,"* as the verse says. We won't fall prey to false doctrine.

I really want to focus, however, on the part that says, *"rightly dividing the word of truth."* When you put the effort into being a diligent studier of your Bible, you will learn to interpret Scripture accurately. *Rightly divide* here literally means to dissect something with a straight, decisive line. It means you will not only learn how to find the correct meanings in Scripture, but when other information comes your way you will compare it accurately against Scripture. In other words, your mind will compare what you have studied and automatically take on the correct point of view. It enables you to dismiss any false or misguided ideas.

THREE KEYS FOR EXPERT BIBLE SKILLS

I also feel it's important to lay out some basics on Bible study. A good handle on the basics is what prepares you to discern the true from the false. With all the different Bible translations and paraphrases, it can be a challenge to get the correct interpretation of Scripture, but by incorporating these guidelines you can become skillful.

There are three key study components needed. Many people don't incorporate all three, but all are necessary for good discernment. Make a point to incorporate the three following:

1. Casual reading

2. Meditating in the Word

3. In-depth study

CASUAL READING

Regular Bible reading helps you get knowledgeable because you get an overview of the events, people involved, and historical timelines. Casual reading helps you see the "big picture" because you are taking in larger pieces of information at one time. We have to remember that the original transcripts of the Bible were not written in chapter and verse, but in passages or as letters, so we should make a point sometimes to read them as such. We use the numbering system today for clarity and referencing. By reading without being constricted by chapter and verse, you'll be surprised at how many times the subject matter doesn't change from chapter to chapter.

MEDITATING ON THE WORD

Meditating is rehearsing what you have read. This would include memorization or what I like to call just "soaking up" the Word of God. This is a good time to repeat and confess Scripture out loud, think on how it applies to you, or just roll it over in your heart and allow it to ignite your faith. Consider meditating on the Word as you pray, drive to work, or simply while you're working throughout the day. Another way I like to meditate on the promises of the Word is by writing or typing Scriptures on index cards. I can tuck these cards in my Bible or purse and pull them out from time to time and speak them aloud to myself.

Meditating on the Word of God solidifies it in your spirit and makes it become real to you. Everyone needs time to just meditate on the Word, because it has a special way of helping you overcome anything. Isn't that what the Lord told Joshua?

> *This book of the law shall not depart out of thy mouth; but thou shalt meditate therein day and night, that thou mayest observe to do according to all that is written therein: for then thou shalt make thy way prosperous, and then thou shalt have good success* (Joshua 1:8).

In other words, speaking and meditating on the Word will empower you to walk it out and the result will be success.

IN-DEPTH STUDY

Everyone needs study time, and this is not just reading someone else's books or watching preaching on television! Those things can certainly enhance a good study routine and help us compare notes and expand revelation. However, we also need time alone with just our Bible and some good reference materials. You need to study, even if you don't consider yourself the studying type. Get several widely-used translations of the Bible or Bible software that contains these and study the meanings of different words in the Bible dictionary or concordance. Look up comparison Scriptures and so forth. There are many guidebooks to give you some study help as well. The idea is to dig deep and draw out hidden revelation in the Bible.

In-depth Bible study is like the man who built a house:

> *He is like a man which built an house, and digged deep, and laid the foundation on a rock: and when the flood arose, the stream beat vehemently upon that house, and could not shake it: for it was founded upon a rock* (Luke 6:48).

What happened to his house? It couldn't be shaken in the storm because he dug his foundation deep! Some revelation in Scripture is hidden because God wants the spiritually hungry ones to be the ones to find it. That is how we discover the treasures of the Kingdom of God (see Matt. 13:44). It is the hungry who go digging for the depths of God who find the precious things of His Spirit. They are the ones who have the most unmovable spiritual foundations.

CORRECTLY INTERPRETING SCRIPTURE

With those three components in place, being able to discern false doctrine from the true also requires knowing how to accurately interpret what you do read and study in the Bible. In other words, you need to know what it means. There are a few rules to interpreting Scripture that we have to incorporate. Because people don't always incorporate them, they get off-track. Sometimes it isn't actual false doctrine they get tangled with, it's just misguided beliefs. The following guidelines will help you study accurately and come away with the correct interpretation:

1. Never try to make the Bible conform to you.

2. Always study the context.

3. Compare Scripture with other Scripture.

4. The Bible is past, present, and future.

5. Scripture contains dual meanings.

6. Point everything to Christ.

7. Study word definitions.

NEVER TRY TO MAKE THE BIBLE CONFORM TO YOU

Some people hear certain teachings and from there get certain doctrines or beliefs stuck in their heads. Therefore, by the time they actually study the subject, they have already determined to make the Bible say something it doesn't. They usually don't intentionally try to change God's Word. What typically happens is they are convinced that the Bible supports what they already know to be "true." Then they study in an effort to support their predetermined conclusion. A lot of people listen more to preaching and opinions about the Bible than actually studying the Bible itself. This is why they are convinced the Bible says what they already know.

Go to the Word of God with an open heart. Take what you have perhaps heard preached and study with a willingness to either change your previous view or strengthen it.

ALWAYS STUDY THE CONTEXT

We mentioned earlier that this is why casual Bible reading is so important. It helps you understand the context. Taking Scripture out of context is one of the biggest contributors to people getting misguided. Always make a point to read the surrounding verses. There are many verses we read a certain way individually, but once read in context we can see the writer was often saying something far beyond what the verse on its own could indicate. For example, look at Second Corinthians:

> *(For the weapons of our warfare are not carnal, but mighty through God to the pulling down of strong holds;) Casting down imaginations, and every high thing that exalteth itself against the knowledge of God, and bringing into captivity every thought to the obedience of Christ* (2 Corinthians 10:4-5).

Often we quote this verse to mean something similar to the following:

"Our spiritual weapons against strongholds are mighty through God, and if we want to be victorious in spiritual warfare we need to take control of every thought and bring it under the obedience of Christ."

Is that basically how you have heard it? Yet if you read the context of the chapter, you will learn that the subject matter was not really much about spiritual warfare itself. Paul was speaking about his apostolic authority to govern the church. The fact that the King James Version places parentheses around verse 4 means it is an inserted thought in a surrounding subject. Just a quick glance at verse 2 begins with Paul saying he might have to use bold authority in dealing with people who were unjustly criticizing his apostleship. He defends himself in verse 3 by saying that even though he was merely human he came with a heavenly authority. Then in verse 4, the word *warfare* means *military service*. Of course this can also mean our service as believers in spiritual warfare. However, Paul used it here to defend his God-given ministerial position. The New Living Translation says, *"We use God's mighty weapons, not worldly weapons, to knock down the strongholds of human reasoning and to destroy false arguments..."* (2 Cor. 10:4 NLT). It was because some were accusing him of unjustly taking his authority, as we see throughout the chapter. *Strong's Concordance* also notes the word *warfare* in verse 4 to mean "apostolic career."[1] In Paul's case, his apostolic ministry was part of his spiritual military service and was the purpose of his warfare in this situation.

Probably the most compelling are verses 5 and 6. In the phrase, *"casting down imaginations,"* Paul was not saying he was trying to cast evil thoughts from the devil out of his mind. Nearly all translations indicate he was saying that he was ready to dispel the thoughts and arguments of speculators against him and make their ideas, particularly about his ministry, conform to Jesus Christ. From there, he says in verse 6 that those who refuse would be disciplined!

Now this isn't to say that the truth of what we have known in verses 4 and 5 is no longer applicable. Paul was still stating a fact. Yes, in any situation, whether it is about our ministerial authority or dealing with other demon powers, we still have mighty weapons of warfare in Christ! And yes, we still *do* need to cast down any imagination or thoughts that rebel against Christ, whether it's false arguments against church leadership, as with Paul, or simply wrong thoughts that arise in our minds.

Nevertheless, we can see why reading in context is important because it opens new revelation. Now that isn't to say certain Scriptures cannot be read by themselves. It just means we need to read verses in light of the subject matter surrounding them. Then, if they actually can stand alone, other Scriptures will also support the truth gleaned from them.

COMPARE SCRIPTURE WITH OTHER SCRIPTURE

When you find what appears to be a truth from Scripture, look for other verses and passages that support your findings. Some people have made the mistake of building whole doctrines on one verse or just a phrase from a verse. For example, if you find a verse about marriage and divorce as you try to find answers on the subject, look for as many verses as possible that cover that subject. Not only will it strengthen your ability to believe what you have read, but it will give you a balanced Bible understanding on it. You will find that each verse will provide another key piece to the puzzle and will help you gain the right doctrinal beliefs. This combined with other rules for interpreting Scripture will open your eyes to the heartbeat of the Holy Spirit on whatever you are studying.

THE BIBLE IS PAST, PRESENT, AND FUTURE

What this means is that the passages of Scripture apply to multiple generations.

One of the biggest examples of Scripture being past, present, and future is in regards to the events of the Book of Revelation. There is resurgence of debate arising over whether some or all of it has already happened or if it is all still in the future. Most have stood by the fact that the events of Revelation are only beginning to come to pass and that most have yet to occur (Futurist and Dispensationalist Theology). Others believe most or all of these events took place in A.D. 70 with the destruction of Jerusalem (Partial or Full Preterism Theology). Another group says many of these events have come to pass, but some are still occurring as the Body of Christ steadily takes dominion, overthrowing satan's kingdom until it makes way for the set-up of Christ's millennial reign (Dominion Theology). Beyond these there are many other variations, and we will touch more on these in the next chapter.

However, we have to know that the Bible speaks to every generation. While many Scriptures were written in reference to the Jews, they also applied to the early Church and still apply today. Even though some cultural or ceremonial practices are no more and the historical settings have changed, these passages still reveal spiritual truths applicable for us now and will hold unique truth for future generations.

With this in mind, it's easier to gain a better understanding on a highly-debated subject like eschatology, or the end times. If the Bible is past, present, and future, there are probably elements of truth to each of the viewpoints I mentioned a moment ago. Of course, keep in mind that elements of truth don't make a doctrine legitimate, they just make it debatable.

Sure, it's reasonably possible that certain or similar events from the Book of Revelation took place in A.D. 70. Since we know that the seven churches existed at that time, it's possible that certain of the listed catastrophic events occurred in the same time frame. However, on the other hand, we also know that most modern-day churches pattern after at least one of those same seven churches in Revelation, but on a wider, global scale. Knowing this, we should also believe that many of the judgments written will also in effect repeat themselves, just as the seven churches appear to have done. Yet, just as the pattern of churches is more worldwide in scale, the disasters would also be on a more magnified global scale. This would realistically point to a future apocalypse.

My point is that we have to treat Scripture as applicable to whatever generation reads it. We always have to ask ourselves the question, "How does this verse or passage apply to us today and apply to me?" The Book of Revelation still has to speak today! I think we can and should take this multiple time period approach to many biblical prophecies in Scripture. Yes, maybe it happened, but it still speaks, and as history repeats itself it is yet to come to pass!

Some of the visions of Daniel and Ezekiel, many will agree, applied to Persia and the surrounding regions of that time. However, many also say the descriptions fit well into the way national events are setting up in modern times. Undoubtedly, those visions will continue to apply to a future yet to unfold.

Think of all the past events that happened to the children of Israel. Sure they happened back then, but look at what the Bible says about them: *"Now these things were our examples, to the intent we should not lust after evil things, as they also lusted"* (1 Cor. 10:6). In other words, what happened to them is still happening in our lives today and will continue to be an issue of importance in future generations.

Solomon stated it so well by saying

> *The thing that hath been, is that which shall be; and*
> *that which is done is that which shall be done: and there*
> *is no new thing under the sun* (Ecclesiastes 1:9).

That is what makes the Word of God so supernatural and living. In a miraculous way it is never outdated, and every word remains amazingly applicable to the present generation. As you study doctrine and interpret the Bible, it is important to always remain aware of this truth because it will help you draw accurate scriptural conclusions.

Never treat the Bible as something that is already past or only applies to the future of someone else. Treat every word as applicable to you personally and applicable to your present generation.

SCRIPTURE CONTAINS DUAL MEANINGS

Just as the Bible can apply to multiple generations, it also can have dual meanings. What I mean by that is that certain passages still have additional hidden truths embedded into them when read in context. Again, my example earlier from Second Corinthians 10:3-6 is a good example. Yes, the passage was about church governmental authority, but the fact is that we still do have mighty spiritual weapons for pulling down strongholds (see Eph. 6:10-18).

Here is an easy way to understand this. When you read or study the Bible, always remember that there are three basic meanings. There is the literal meaning, the historical meaning, and the prophetic or symbolic meaning.

In Paul's example from Second Corinthians 10, the *historical* setting was that he had many problems overall in dealing with the church of Corinth. The *literal* lesson found in the verses is about Paul's apostleship and church government issues. But beyond those we can still find *prophetic* insight embedded there about spiritual warfare, taking control of our thoughts, and so on.

The Old Testament is one of the best places to glean dual meanings from Scripture. One example is from the Book of Joel. *Historically*, the book discussed the sin and disobedience happening in Zion at the time. In the historical meaning you could also learn a lot about Israel's background, which would help you understand other Scripture. The *literal* truth found is a lesson on God's judgment of sin, repentance, and so on.

But you can draw *prophetic* meaning from Joel that also points to the future church and spiritual warfare. For example, Joel 2:10 and

30-31 talk about the sun and moon being darkened as God's judgment is released. This scenario is repeated in Acts 2:19-20 and shows us the characteristics of the Spirit of God moving on the Church as they stand as His army filled with the Holy Spirit. Prophetically, the descriptions of the army in Joel 2 could certainly be applicable to the kind of warrior God wants every believer in His army to be.

Once again, when it comes to the end times and eschatology, you should still see the historical, literal, and symbolic meanings. Some debate the legitimacy of the thousand-year millennial reign of Christ. Some believe it is literal (Premillennialism Theology), and others say it is only a symbol of the fact that Christ already reigns through the Church until the world is judged (Amillennialism Theology).

However, the supernatural beauty of interpreting Scripture is that both have certain truthful applications. Literally speaking, Scripture warns us to prepare our lives daily for Christ's return and points to a literal reign on earth for one thousand years (see 2 Pet. 3:13-14). My feeling is that if there are literal catastrophes, then there must be a literal reign as well. But symbolically and prophetically you can also draw a safe conclusion that Christ's Kingdom is already reigning in the heart of every Christian, and all who promote the Gospel are in fact expanding the Kingdom today (see Luke 17:20-21).

Of course, these are just a few examples. Where possible, try to gain a basic understanding of all three meanings of Scripture and apply them all. Remember, *the Bible tells history, it is always literal in nature, but it imparts prophetic insight.* This mindset will help you gain a clearer view, making it harder to misinterpret things.

POINT EVERYTHING TO CHRIST

Another rule for interpreting Scripture is to understand that Jesus Christ is the center of all Scripture from Genesis to Revelation. Everything in some way points back to Him. The entire

Old Covenant practices were only shadows of a new and better Covenant yet to come in Christ (see Heb. 8:6). The writings of the prophets point to Christ. The prophecies of Revelation and Daniel point to Christ. The stories of Abraham, Isaac, and Jacob point to Christ. Moses and the Exodus is a typology of Christ, and so on. Jesus Christ has been given the scepter of heavenly rule, and He is the Lord of all (see Heb. 1:8)! So when you interpret Scripture, everything must ultimately relate to Christ, His death, and His glorious resurrection.

For example, do you know why you cannot take Old Testament Scriptures on polygamy and make a doctrine out of them? That is because, in the New Testament under Christ's Lordship, polygamy was never endorsed by church leadership and the practice was abolished. Globally today, nearly all civilized cultures reject the practice of polygamy, because after the Cross there was a new mindset deposited in humanity.

The same was true with animal sacrifice under Judaism. Jesus' blood replaced it. Interestingly, after Jesus arose, God saw to it that the system of animal sacrifice was abolished and is no longer practiced today. In fact, blood sacrifices by any group globally today are usually considered cultic and in most cases illegal. There is a dramatic difference between b.c. and a.d. Never forget that. If you look at all Scripture through the power and resurrection of Jesus Christ, you will gain a vivid understanding of why certain things were written in the Bible and why they are a certain way today.

STUDY WORD DEFINITIONS

Because the Bible we read today is a translation of the original, we need to make sure we study words for clarity. My husband and I travel a lot to foreign nations, and I have learned how much can get lost in translation. While God has watched over His Word to make sure its meaning is protected, we are still subject to the many translations and paraphrases that all vary somewhat from the original.

Make a point to compare translations until you find a common meaning of certain words and phrases. I like to make notes on these words and sometimes even write the meanings directly in my Bible. For some people, the King James Version is too hard to comprehend and they get lost when reading it. I agree that the older phrases found in some of the more traditional translations can be a challenge. On the other hand, some of the newer translations and paraphrases are almost too trendy and have lost some of the original meaning and some have even omitted key texts. Personally, I use the King James and then prefer to use other translations for comparison.

Many people have misinterpreted Scripture because they mistook the meaning of a word, thinking it meant one thing when it really meant something else. I have seen entire doctrines and sermons built on a mistaken word definition.

There has been a bit of a new trend these days in some church groups that negates the need for in-depth word study. Now, they don't come right out and say, "Don't study the Greek and Hebrew." They say things like, "How many of you know we don't have to get caught up in the Greek and Hebrew all the time?" I certainly understand the need not to become a bunch of dried-up professors who pour so deeply over Bible definitions that we lose all sense of liveliness in the Spirit. However, we also can't become so hip and modern that we equally lose the important need for in-depth study of God's Word that is needed in order to gain its true meaning.

CHARACTERISTICS OF DANGEROUS DOCTRINES

Armed with just a few of the basic skills needed for Bible study and interpretation, we should now explore some of the characteristics seen in the doctrines of danger.

Keep in mind there is a difference between dangerous doctrines of error and simple human mistakes. All of us are growing in our understanding and can make mistakes in how we understand revelation. It is important not to mistakenly reject good leaders or even fellow believers on what we thought to be false doctrine when it was really a simple misinterpretation or even a lack of understanding on our own part. Sometimes we reject and even discredit when we only heard pieces of information. Had we waited for more it might have helped us get a different view. Also, many people and preachers say things they later wish they hadn't. Make sure before you label something as "false" that you have taken some serious time to weigh out the facts and information.

On the flip side, there are those who *have* made a commitment to believe and teach dangerous and erroneous doctrines. If you remember my story in Chapter Three about the ministry couple we met who decided to go down the road of false doctrine, there were not only several signs that a seducing spirit was present, but there was also clear evidence of false doctrine.

From this, I learned that just as there are warning signs of seducing spirits, there are also certain characteristics present in dangerous false doctrines. Of course, if you are a diligent student of the Word, as I have been saying repeatedly, you will be better prepared to ward off any error. However, in addition to that it is good to look for certain characteristics common to error. If you hear teaching and doctrine that you are unsure of but most or all of the signs listed here are *not* prevalent, then perhaps it is just a simple human error. Here are some characteristics common to false doctrine:

1. It never gains wide acceptance and momentum.

2. It appeals mostly to the nonconformists.

3. There is an emphasis on extremes.

4. The source and character of those involved is questionable.

5. There is an emphasis on unusual supernatural manifestations.

6. There is a denial of the foundational basics.

7. There is a lack of anointing.

IT NEVER GAINS WIDE ACCEPTANCE AND MOMENTUM

Typically, like history, most false doctrines repeat themselves. They come around again from time to time, sometimes under different names. Every few years, they make their way around Christendom again through certain groups who are determined to promote them. They come in many different forms with varying views but never gain wide acceptance. Some are more common in Charismatic circles, and others are more adapted among evangelicals. Nonetheless, look at the history and do some research. Has this doctrine come up before in decades gone by? Has it been around for a while and never seems to have gone anywhere? Does it rise up with a sudden surge for a short period and then dissipate into the background again?

Even though there are those who are committed to them, I believe there is a reason certain doctrines never prosper and only a select few accept them. It is because the Holy Spirit is not endorsing them.

For example, many groups since the Azuza Street Revival denied speaking in tongues as the evidence of the baptism of the Holy Spirit. Others have only acknowledged its very limited use, while others have rejected the entire existence of speaking in tongues altogether in the modern-day Church. However, regardless of some rejection, the

Charismatic and Pentecostal movement continues to be the fastest-growing worldwide Christian movement on the planet. I believe this is undoubtedly because the Holy Spirit is behind it, and that is why it has prospered so powerfully.

The best biblical example of doctrine succeeding on a wide scale is when the apostles of the early Church were being persecuted in Acts 5. A Pharisee named Gamaliel made a powerful statement about them. He said:

> *Then stood there up one in the council, a Pharisee, named Gamaliel, a doctor of the law, had in reputation among all the people, and commanded to put the apostles forth a little space; And said unto them, Ye men of Israel, take heed to yourselves what ye intend to do as touching these men. For before these days rose up Theudas, boasting himself to be somebody; to whom a number of men, about four hundred, joined themselves: who was slain; and all, as many as obeyed him, were scattered, and brought to nought. After this man rose up Judas of Galilee in the days of the taxing, and drew away much people after him: he also perished; and all, even as many as obeyed him, were dispersed. And now I say unto you, Refrain from these men, and let them alone: for if this counsel or this work be of men, it will come to nought: But if it be of God, ye cannot overthrow it; lest haply ye be found even to fight against God* (Acts 5:34-39).

What happened here to the ones who were not from God? They died! Their efforts perished and were destroyed. On the other hand, those who were from God could not be stopped. Be wary of camps, groups, and doctrines that after a period of time, even with effort, never seem to gain momentum on any reasonable level.

IT APPEALS MOSTLY TO THE NONCONFORMISTS

I am wary of doctrines that appeal mostly to the people or groups who feel they are always rejected, dejected, or just motivated by special interests. They are so deeply looking for something that finally gives them a feeling of acceptance that they ignore all sound reason in order to participate. This is why many teenagers join street gangs. They are looking for a place to belong or gain a feeling of superiority. The devil has his eye on people in this category.

False doctrines always seem to be surrounded by the mavericks. They are often those who can't maintain normal relationships. In them you find the socially introverted and those who feel hurt by life, had a painful experience, or never received proper emotional fulfillment. Some gravitate toward it because they need that kind of platform in order to make something of themselves. Often they get involved because that circle gave them some twisted form of self-confidence.

If you examine the personalities of some of the world's greatest dictators and cult leaders, you will find this nonconformist personality in all of them. There is something wrong with people who can't seem to agree with anything or anyone. They always have a problem with everything and every teaching and they need a place to promote "their thing." From that, we find people who feel they are the only one who has received a particular revelation, and they walk around as self-promoting loners.

Now let me clarify—that doesn't mean every time someone goes against the grain they should automatically be labeled among the false. Many things from God started out of controversy as we even see in the ministry of Jesus and the early Church. God also raised up

Martin Luther and many other reformists to speak a divine message, but Martin Luther's message *eventually* received worldwide acceptance and is preached today as one of the foundational truths of Christianity.

We also cannot label people nonconformists simply because they are not part of our familiar denomination, circle, ministry network, or camp. What makes a true nonconformist is when they can't conform to *anything* or anyone that is considered legitimate in the Body of Christ. They can only seem to conform to themselves.

THERE IS AN EMPHASIS ON EXTREMES

False doctrines can also be marked by excesses. These usually include the most unusual clothing or fashion requirements, overly demanding lifestyles, or stringent religious rituals. Many of these impose such extreme rule that those involved can hardly have a normal lifestyle. Others are so lax that participants have lost any real fear of God. Sometimes you find a bizarre mixture of both, often with stringent rules regarding religious ceremonies but no expected standards for private morals or vice versa.

Of course, we are commonly aware of these issues among some of the most extreme cults. However, we are less aware of them when it comes to some that are a little closer to our doorstep. Many of these inch right within our Charismatic churches and almost always include some idea within their creeds about the future or eternity. Either they promote extreme fear and paranoia or an excessive feeling of peace and safety. Nearly all false doctrines have some extreme emphasis that applies to one of these two categories.

For example, some are busy prophesying with their last breath that God is about to strike California and it will fall into the Pacific Ocean any day now, so they are busy preparing by collecting cans of beans in their basement. Others believe there will be little to no serious catastrophic events, expecting our days to only get brighter as the Church eventually overcomes every tidbit of evil on the planet. Some have just decided God loves everybody so much that there is no possible way there can be punishment for anyone either in this life or in eternity.

Look for these kinds of extremes and excesses when exploring doctrine. It always is a factor in some way, and usually a portion of the emphasis is on the future events.

THE SOURCE AND CHARACTER OF THOSE INVOLVED IS QUESTIONABLE

Second Peter 2 has a great deal to say about false prophets and teachers. However, the focus is particularly on their background and character. We couldn't even begin to list here all the negative character traits of the false teachers found in this chapter, and there are many other chapters that describe similar traits.

We find that Scripture places a large emphasis on their lifestyle, affiliations, relationships, and preaching patterns. Do they run with a rare, select few, or are they part of a legitimate group or network? Does their preaching always focus on one narrow viewpoint or specific extreme? You should also be able to tell after listening to them long enough if they exhibit a godly persona or if they are just strange. In many cases, false doctrines are marked by "justified" immoral behaviors.

Often people ignore all the signals about certain people or groups, even when something about them seems "off." Look for preachers with proven fruit who exhibit the signs of having right character. Also look for the ones whose ministries have stood the test of time. If they are newer to the ministry scene, note who they are connected with and watch their character to see what fruit comes from their ministry.

UNUSUAL SUPERNATURAL MANIFESTATIONS

Another common characteristic of false doctrines are not only extreme beliefs and requirements, but many of them are marked by unusual supernatural manifestations. We have all heard about cults that were started by a person who received a "revelation" through some strange angelic visitation or similar bizarre occurrence.

Now, I am all for the supernatural power of God, but it *must* maintain its basis within Scripture, especially the common pattern of practice within the New Testament. Additionally, any revelation received from a supernatural manifestation must line up with the Bible.

I think the best way to stay on track when it comes to supernatural things is to look at the ministry of Jesus and the early church and the kind of manifestations they usually emulated. Most of their supernatural manifestations were focused around physical healing or miracles and deliverance from evil spirits. While there *were* other types of manifestations at times, healing and deliverance were the most *emphasized*.

There were also other unusual situations beyond that, such as when Phillip was translated. I have no problem if someone is translated today, particularly for the purpose of preaching of the Gospel, since that manifestation is in the Bible and it did happen to a New Testament believer (see Acts 8:26-40). But I would have trouble making that a commonly expected type of manifestation because it wasn't common in Scripture. In fact, Phillip's case happened surrounding his encounter of ministry to the eunuch, who served under Candace, the Queen of Ethiopia. This event historically opened all of Ethiopia to the Gospel and still has impact to this day. Nonetheless, supernatural translation was a rare occurrence and is recorded in no other cases to aid in the early church's ministry endeavors. When it did happen in Phillip's case, it had a very large national and historical impact.

Yet some groups today are taking a manifestation such as this or similar unusual manifestations and turning them into some kind of regular practice or "ministry." They are placing a heavy emphasis on these types of things.

Placing emphasis on things the Bible doesn't is often a clue that something has gotten offtrack. Lately, some camps within Charismatic circles are getting tilted the wrong way by overemphasizing extreme manifestations that the Bible didn't place an emphasis upon. They are mixing the genuine with the false, and the whole thing is becoming adulterated. Sure, some of these occurrences may be in the Bible, but they weren't a New Testament pattern to deliberately emulate. Some are even taking it to the next level of now "manifesting" things that are not even biblical.

I struggle with some of the manifestations circulating in the church today that include things such as money appearing from nowhere, oil or blood coming from people's skin, images of Jesus appearing in a cookie, or unusual forms of "angels" or other supernatural beings visiting people. Along the lines of being translated, many are now claiming to "travel" through spiritual dimensions. Of course, there are countless other examples.

As of late, some have even gone so far to say that they have received visitations from dead saints during spiritual visions! In effort to have the supernatural, I think these groups are getting into unbiblical and even dangerous extremes that must be sharply discerned.

We only find two Bible examples of people interacting with dead saints. One was Saul who called up Samuel through the use of witchcraft and of course lost his kingdom immediately afterward. So obviously that wouldn't be an example for us to follow. That serves as a warning of something *not* to do! Second was the example of Jesus on the Mount of Transfiguration when He spoke with Moses and Elijah. Most agree that was a special occurrence specifically unique to the eternal supremacy of Christ and prophetic history. So I wouldn't tread on making that a biblical example one can use either. Furthermore, the Bible warns clearly against talking to the dead, even if they *were* a Bible figure (Deut. 18:10-11). That would be why we find *no* examples of the early Christians or any church leaders in the New Testament having such an experience as talking to or "receiving something" from a dead saint.

Additionally, we need to be discerning against strange manifestations such as those who talk to angels that arrive in the form of something different than how angels appeared to people in the Bible. The only form of angel that visited and interacted with anyone in Scripture came in the appearance of what was described to resemble a *male* human. They weren't unusual creatures or females. They weren't flashing lights or other objects. The Seraphim, Cherubim, and unusual creatures seen in the visions of the Bible prophets never visited and interacted with humans on earth. They surrounded the Throne and were only witnessed by these prophets in visions. These weren't visitations in which they interacted or talked with them, nor did they receive any kind of "impartation" or "calling" from them. The one the prophets spoke with was the Lord, and the actual visitation came from the Spirit of the Lord and Him alone.

When an angelic visitor actually spoke to people, the Bible reveals that it always resembled a male, human form. Additionally, it is also interesting to note that outside of the Revelation of John, the early church members had no such extreme visions. While visions are for us today, we need to stay with the types of visions the Bible emphasizes. We need to be moderate about the more unusual things.

Some regularly claim that money or other valuable substances appear from nowhere. Actually, this kind of "manifestation" has circulated in Christendom for years and resurfaces every now and then. Again, some base its legitimacy on the account when Jesus took the coin from the fish's mouth to pay taxes. But again, this was not a *common practice* on Jesus' part, nor do we see it ever happen to the early apostles. In fact, we know Jesus had a treasury bag, and we have no record of money ever supernaturally appearing in it.

It is also necessary to realize that many of the other uncommon miracles of Jesus—such as the time He turned water to wine, walked on water, or fed the multitudes—carried certain prophetic meanings that were specific to Jesus Himself. In other words, they happened to reveal a key prophetic truth about His Lordship and supremacy. They weren't meant to be a pattern for us to emulate or Jesus would have emphasized such practices for the apostles to follow.

For example, I believe when Jesus fed the multitudes it prophetically represented that Jesus had come to distribute *Himself* as the bread of life for the multitudes of the world. Now, at the same time I have also heard many powerful stories of missionaries or people in desperate circumstances when food wasn't readily available who actually had food multiply in some unusual way. But again, the multiplication of food wasn't a New Testament ministry pattern or emphasis that would be emulated in a church service or conference. That means we shouldn't make it the focus or a pattern to promote among those we preach to, but rather focus on the God who will readily meet our need in dire situations. He can and will do that supernaturally or however He chooses if we trust Him and expect Him to meet our needs.

Additionally, when Jesus turned water into wine, it was undoubtedly a representation of the baptism and infilling of the Holy Spirit. Could the Lord change one substance into another? Of course, the Lord can do that! Still, we simply don't see the early church ministries emulating the practice. This indicates that we also shouldn't make a practice of these unusual occurrences. We need to stay with the overall biblical practice. Yet, there are ministries making the majority of their focus on such manifestations.

The Bible always seems to draw the attention of the supernatural mostly back to deliverance and healing, and all manifestations were specifically pointed to win souls or happened for those who were committed to winning souls. This was, again, the *emphasis* Jesus gave the apostles when he commissioned them to preach in Matthew 10. He told them to heal the sick and cast out devils. There was no mention of unusual creatures appearing, translations or "spiritual traveling," money appearances, or similar unusual things. We simply don't see these practices as a part of the New Testament pattern which we are to mimic and practice on a regular basis.

On the other hand, I do think the supernatural manifestations of visions and dreams are to be expected and embraced more regularly because the New Testament *emphasizes* them as a common occurrence in the last days among God's people (see Acts 2:17-18). Because of this, we should welcome visions and dreams as being an integral part to getting the Gospel preached. The part we have to discern is—what is revealed or imparted from those visions, and are they unusually extreme in nature? What is received from them needs to line up with Bible doctrine.

That isn't to say that all manifestations will exactly mimic every Bible example, and there are many unusual manifestations that are legitimately from God. However, they *do* need to fall in line with the general emphasis of Scripture and shouldn't receive so much attention that people start to make a common practice of them or build ministry efforts on them. Of course, manifestations that are outright unbiblical should be avoided altogether, particularly those we mentioned earlier such as talking to the dead or strange creatures.

We need to use biblical discernment as these supernatural things get presented more commonly in the last days. The Bible is clear that satan has the power to deceive people through very real lying signs and wonders (see 2 Thess. 2:9). In an effort to have the supernatural, some have gotten over into the false, the New Age practices, and even for some they are manufacturing a lie. As we discern false doctrine, we also need to watch for the extreme or over-emphasized manifestations of the unusual supernatural. This is because demons will most assuredly use these things to make the false things look very believable.

DENIAL OF THE FOUNDATIONAL BASICS

While denominations, ministry networks, camps, and circles can all vary in certain beliefs, most are aligned on the basics such as the resurrection of Jesus, the virgin birth, eternal judgment, and so on. We can disagree on whether or not you can pray in tongues in a church service, but we cannot deviate on the truth of the shed blood of Jesus. False doctrines often have some deviation from one of the basic foundations, the most common and subtle being the ones that deviate on eternal judgment and eternity.

Of course, deviating from foundational truths isn't true in every case. I have heard of churches who believe in bringing rattlesnakes to church to prove the power of God! Sure, maybe they don't deny the virgin birth, but I can tell you that snake handling on the altar ain't from God! That would fall under the category of extremes! However, I still wouldn't be surprised if there isn't some foundational belief they have altered too.

The biblical foundations of our Christian faith should not be arguable. Every Christian should have some solid basic Bible understanding on these foundational truths, so they can recognize when doctrines deviate from the truths in the slightest way. These unalterable foundational truths are:

- The one true God or Trinity of God

- The deity of Jesus Christ

- The virgin birth

- The death and physical resurrection of Jesus

- Universal sin

- Salvation by grace through faith

- The second coming of Christ

- Resurrection of the dead and eternal judgment

- The Bible is the inerrant Word of God

Here are a few examples of false statements out there today that deviate from our foundational truths. They are things like:

- "God could be a female; no one can be sure."

- "Christ wasn't sinless; He was married and/or was not the Son of God."

- "There is no literal hell or eternal punishment because a loving God wouldn't send anyone to hell."

- "Christ isn't literally coming again because He's already come and is here now."

- "We are all children of God, even those who don't believe in Jesus."

- "The Holy Spirit is just a force of energy in the atmosphere."

- "The Bible has inconsistencies and was only created by man."

These are just a small few, but anything along these lines should immediately alert your spirit because they deviate from our basic foundational truths! Run from them; they are not from God!

THERE IS LACK OF AN ANOINTING

If something is from the Lord, the anointing will be upon it. I remember when I was first introduced to the things of the Holy Spirit. I went to my first, big Charismatic conference and remember seeing people lift their hands in worship to the Lord for the first time. I remember wondering what they were doing exactly, since some would just raise only one hand, similar to how you would when raising a hand to alert the teacher in a classroom. There were many other things that happened in that meeting that I didn't understand, like the preacher touching someone on the head and the person falling down! It was new to me.

The only thing I can't forget is that I felt something draw me. It wasn't curiosity, and I knew it wasn't any kind of compulsion. No, it was the best jumping up and down feeling deep inside my stomach that I had ever felt! I loved it! It gave me the most peaceful feeling I had ever known. I *knew* it was from the Lord.

Look for the anointing. Yes, when something is new to you, it may make your mind wonder as you try to sort it all out, but look for that feeling deep down on the inside that you can't get away from. Even when God's presence convicts you of sin and your fleshly humanity wants to run and hide from it, you still *know* it is just what you need! That is the anointing.

On the other hand, when something is *not* from God, look for that churning feeling deep within that feels all wrong. Something gives you that sense that there is something you need to get away from in order to protect yourself. Perhaps it is just a feeling that hangs there like a dark, ominous cloud. In some cases it's just that everything about it feels forced.

In some situations, we can be confused as to whether those feelings are the anointing or just our own personal opinions and preconceived ideas. A good way to discern the difference is through time.

Don't just reject a preacher altogether because you heard one thing you didn't like, unless it was a blatant deviation from foundational truth. If he or she is well respected or has a legitimate ministry, give them time. Sometimes we struggle to find the anointing because of previous experiences and ideas. Listen a while, and whatever spirit is upon them will become more pronounced. Then trust that the Holy Spirit will lead and guide you into all truth (see John 16:13). If you have been putting the right principles of discernment to practice, you won't go down a wrong path.

Keep using the right tools to help you discern doctrine and work hard to have accuracy in interpreting Scripture. Every person who makes an effort to test what they hear against what they know from the Bible will avoid dangerous doctrines, whether blatant or subtle. Believe me, this will be one of your most important assets as a Christian in the last days.

Chapter Six

DISCERNING THE DOCTRINES AND TRENDS TOWARD "PEACE AND SAFETY"

For when they shall say, Peace and safety;
then sudden destruction cometh upon them,
as travail upon a woman with child; and
they shall not escape (1 Thessalonians 5:3).

"Just as I am, without one plea," were the words to the familiar old hymn. Many recall the melody as it was sung by George Beverly Shea in the days of the Billy Graham crusades in which thousands would run to the altar and commit their lives to Jesus Christ. "No one is promised tomorrow," the famous evangelist would say. "Are you ready to meet the Lord if you were to die tonight?" he would ask.

This familiar style of calling people to the altar of repentance was not uncommon, particularly in those days. Preachers, evangelists, and pastors everywhere would preach the reality of eternity, the imminent return of Christ, and the truth of a tormenting hell until listeners would search their souls and make a decision toward salvation. While perhaps not all who responded to this type of salvation call became long-term, committed Christians, the preaching at least caused them to search the condition of their souls.

Many other preachers would take their message to the next level and preach a sacrificial commitment to holy living with intense fervor. They were not afraid to make their listeners shun any idea of getting outside of God's blessing or perhaps even fear spending eternity in hell.

Of course, these days the persona of the classic hellfire and brimstone preacher has faded somewhat, almost making it a thing of the past in many regions. Sure, perhaps in some regards we needed to grow beyond the red-in-the-face, ignited preaching delivery, but somehow we seem to have lost the sobering side of the Gospel message that came with it.

There appears to be a new trend on our horizons that we must discern. It is a trend toward all things being about self-help, prosperity, and personal happiness. It's an obsession of sorts, where everyone is looking for a personal "peace and safety" experience. In fact, the secular world is entirely caught up in this fad. Everywhere you turn is another self-help seminar, a new idea for personal betterment, a workout program, or a plan for stress management.

The church has followed suit in many ways. A great deal of preaching today has become motivational in its approach. In fact, some pastors and preachers are content to be seen as nothing more than motivational speakers. The vast majority of subjects are designed to excite or uplift listeners almost to the point that few sobering truths are mentioned. It's all become about "how you can make it." Sermons are mostly about how to feel better about yourself and take control of your life. There is less room for the convicting power of the Holy Spirit that commands us to conform to the Kingdom of God.

At conferences and conventions, speakers feel the increasing need to deliver only the things that get the people shouting, otherwise they might not be a conference favorite. Pastors have created a church environment that makes people feel so relaxed and good about themselves when they come to church that fewer are realizing the necessary sacrificial commitments required in order to enter the Kingdom. Jesus said that the path into the Kingdom is not an easy path, but a narrow one (see Matt. 7:13-14). A form of Christianity is increasingly being offered without any biblical boundaries.

Personally, however, I was never a fan of churches that drag people to the altar of repentance every week. I have been in those churches more than once, and many have placed too much attention on the need for self-examination. However, lately the trend has gone so far the other way that church attendees and listeners have begun to almost reject the idea of ever having to search their own hearts. In fact, many feel offended if the pastor expects them to do so.

As we grow in our spiritual discernment, I want to focus in this chapter on the ideals, doctrines, and modern-day mindsets that desire to keep us so comfortable that we are in danger of being found asleep when the Bridegroom comes. Mark 13:36 says, *"Lest coming suddenly He find you sleeping."* The context surrounding this verse talks about the need for us to be in a constant state of preparedness for the coming of Jesus Christ.

While sermons, books, and teachings that help people better themselves are definitely necessary, we also need resources that provoke us to think. Not every sermon must include it, but our attention cannot entirely exclude subjects that address eternity or the sobering biblical expectations for true Christianity. I am wary of preaching and resources that give the constant impression that believers have all the time in the world to work out their lives. Some are going so far as to imply that the future on earth holds nothing to be seriously concerned with. At least, many are simply leaving out any content pertinent to God's correction, judgment, or eternal impact.

I believe that in keeping with good discernment we should make sure that our churches, books, programs, and other resources include a strong sense of spiritual awareness along these lines. Again, I want to reiterate that this doesn't mean we have to become caught up in end-time hyper-sensationalism as we often saw in many church circles over past decades. That is probably one reason many pastors and Christians shy away from discussing the reality of the future and anything that touches on end-time issues. However, the opposite extreme of a constant focus toward "peace and safety" usually ignores several important spiritual necessities.

As we remain sharp as Christians, it is necessary that we be on the lookout for the mindsets and ideals that overemphasize our own spiritual and personal comfort. For the remainder of the chapter, I want to discuss a few of the most common ideals being seen as of late.

NO SPIRITUAL READINESS

The committed Christian should live every day preparing for eternity. It would be cumbersome to spend time here listing all the Scriptures that admonish us to do so. We read countless Scriptures that use words like, *watch, be sober, give diligence, awake from sleep, endure to the end,* and so on. The entire New Testament is filled with these types of verses! The Bible is trying to tell us to be ready for the future and live in a constant state of spiritual readiness.

I feel particularly concerned lately about the resurgence of end-time doctrines that diminish the focus away from a future judgment on earth. It seems another method for peace and personal comfort to be the favored line of thinking. These ideals are subtly and conveniently helping believers feel more relaxed. How cunning it would be for the devil to lull Christians into thinking all is well when their own souls are hanging in the balance.

All of Second Peter 3 speaks clearly along these lines. Really, it is important to consider reading the context of the entire chapter, but for now let's refer to some key verses:

> *Most importantly, I want to remind you that in the last days scoffers will come, mocking the truth and following their own desires. They will say, "What happened to the promise that Jesus is coming again? From before the times of our ancestors, everything has remained the same since the world was first created." They deliberately forget that God made the heavens by the word of His command, and He brought the earth out from the water and surrounded it with water. Then He used the water to destroy the ancient world with a mighty flood. And by the same word, the present heavens and earth have been stored up for fire. They are being kept for the day of judgment, when ungodly people will be destroyed. But you must not forget this one thing, dear friends: A day is like a thousand years to the Lord, and a thousand years is like a day* (2 Peter 3:3-8 NLT).

Basically, these verses are saying that we can't be found among those who make it seem as if Jesus isn't coming back any time soon, if at all. Sure, there are many in the secular world who purposefully mock the return of Christ, and these Scriptures are most certainly referring to them. However, there are also many in the church these days who are no longer promoting the firm belief in Christ's return to judge the world. This thought is having a growing popularity among many Charismatics. Some are beginning to touch on things that give the idea that a sudden return of Christ according to the widely-accepted belief is probably not an accurate assessment. Others are simply ignoring it while their sermons become more geared toward a motivational approach.

According to this passage of Scripture, however, this present earth is being kept in its current state only until the dramatic Day of Judgment when all ungodliness on the earth will be destroyed. These verses make it clear that this time of judgment on earth will be in conjunction with the return of Christ. Verse 8 encourages us not to begin wondering if and when it will happen, but to remain aware that *it will* happen soon. For what we think might be a long time away may be closer than we realize, because a thousand years in our minds is like one day to the Lord. That means our calendar thinking is often very different from God's. The message here is that we should be spiritually ready at any hour. The only reason God has delayed the time is because He wants as many as possible to come to repentance (see 2 Peter 3:9).

If you look further, it says:

> *Seeing then that all these things shall be dissolved, what manner of persons ought ye to be in all holy conversation and godliness* (2 Peter 3:11).

There is growing popularity that deviates from the line of thinking in this verse. It's causing a new interest in end-time doctrines that are less focused on the need for spiritual readiness. While most of them are not new, they have resurged as of late and are gaining more popularity in a Christian world that wants a more pleasing, "self-help" type of Gospel. Most of these doctrinal ideals have been rejected by the mainline church. However, combined with a Christian world that is increasingly desirous of obtaining personal fulfillment, it seems these kinds of doctrines are receiving more interest among some of the mainline Christians and preachers.

It isn't my intent to spend time trying to dispel all the arguments on them, because that isn't the purpose of this book. What I want you to see is a common thread that we have to discern. It is a trend toward all things of "peace and safety." Of course, this is just a short list of modern doctrines that tend to imply it, and there are many varying views on them. However, my goal is to help you see how this "peace and safety" mindset would love to seep into our thinking. I want us to discern today's tendency toward a false sense of peace.

FULL PRETERISM

It's been around in various forms for a long time but is on the rise again. This doctrine states that the typical Scriptures used in end-time teachings have either all come to pass or mostly have come to pass. This includes the Book of Revelation, the prophecies of Daniel, and those of Jesus, such as in Matthew 24. Full preterists believe that these things all took place in A.D. 70 with the destruction of Jerusalem, as I mentioned before. Partial preterists believe some of them took place.

After hearing some views on Full Preterism, I made a point to read the Book of Revelation and many of the eschatological Scriptures again. I couldn't help but shudder with awe as I read the pages. When I study doctrine, I ask the Holy Spirit to show me things through the anointing. I must say that I felt the presence of God on the prophecies of Revelation and can't help but know that those prophecies speak to us of things yet to come. The words thunder from the pages with force! I can't deviate from the "global" terminology used through-out the book, which I believe the Holy Spirit deliberately intended.

Preterists try to assert that these things were confined to the region of the Middle East, but the worldwide, global language used throughout Revelation begs otherwise. Perhaps to the apostle John, the world from his view in the middle eastern regions meant "all the earth," but undoubtedly the Holy Spirit meant all the earth by looking at the entire planet.

Again, I have to reiterate a point I already made in previous chapters. Remember, the Bible always has a literal and a prophetic message, not only applicable to a past generation, but also applicable to the current generation. Not only is it historically literal, but it is also remains literal in the present time and future. Not only did passages such as Matthew 24 speak directly to the Jews and Jesus' disciples, they are also applicable to us as Christians today.

If it were strictly a reference to A.D. 70 and a message for the Jews of that day, then what's the point of reading and applying Jesus' message now? It most certainly has application for us today and it speaks of events that *are* obviously happening before our very eyes. We would have to be blind not to notice. This further proves that it is speaking of future events still to come.

While the passage references events specific to Jerusalem, again the terminology is very global and worldwide in its approach. The way many events are described can realistically only point to something still to come because the earth has *never literally* experienced the freakish events of nature that the Bible describes. Placing it all in the past forces you to read these events only as prophetic typologies that have no literal impact on modern life. The worldwide cataclysmic nature of the events described simply makes these occurrences too vast for the small region surrounding the Middle East. I've heard arguments otherwise, and while very creative, they simply don't stand up to the most basic rules for interpreting Scripture. *The Bible must always apply to the present generation.* If it doesn't, then there is little point to following it.

This is one of the biggest loopholes in preterist thinking. To make the idea work, they have to stand by the belief that the books or letters of the New Testament were only specifically relevant to the generation they were written to and claim these verses were never addressing anything literal to us who live in the present. Some even use First and Second Timothy as an example, stating that it was strictly a conversation between Timothy and Paul. A person could say that about any book of the Bible if they wanted, but then this makes the Bible irrelevant to us. While some cultural things found in the New Testament may have changed, the truths, warnings, and admonishments embedded must still apply.

I will argue one last point against preterist thought, even though there are many to contend with. Probably the most common verse they use is Matthew 16:28, which says, *"Verily I say unto you, There be some standing here, which shall not taste of death, till they see the Son of Man coming in His kingdom."* In short, preterists use this verse to say, "Jesus must have come back during the apostles' lifetime, because Jesus promised the apostles they wouldn't all die before Jesus came."

However, the word *see* in this verse is the word *eido,* which we reviewed in Chapter Four in reference to the woman at the well. It means "to see, have a revelation or divine perception."[1] Jesus wasn't telling them that in their lifetime they were going to literally participate in Jesus' return to earth. He was telling them that they were going to get a divine understanding of what it will be like when the Son of Man reigns majestically in His Kingdom.

In addition, the word *coming* in the verse is the word *erchomai.* It simply means "to come" or "*a* coming."[2] In Acts 7:52 it is used to reference Jesus' first coming to earth to be crucified. It doesn't imply a long-abiding presence, but rather an appearance. Notably the word "coming" here isn't the word *parousia* which is the word for "come" that references Jesus' continual abiding presence and is often used biblically in reference to Jesus' literal second coming. *Parousia* means to come and to stay—an abiding presence.[3] Presently, we have Jesus' presence in the person of the Holy Spirit, but not His abiding presence as the reigning King of Majesty as he showed the disciples on the Mount of Transfiguration.

When Jesus told the disciples they would *"see the Son of Man coming,"* He was saying they would have a divine revelation through a supernatural appearance. Then immediately after that, they experienced the Mount of Transfiguration in Matthew 17. In fact, no place other than the Mount of Transfiguration do we find the apostles witnessing any "coming" of Jesus in that kind of majestic power. That is because His literal coming on that level hasn't happened yet; Jesus only wanted to give them a picture.

In other words, you could say that Jesus "came" *(erchomai)* or appeared to the apostles so they would "see" *(eido)* and receive a divine revelation of Jesus' majestic Kingdom yet to come. There are many more points on this subject, but Second Peter gives more clarity. It says:

> *For we were not following cleverly devised stories when we made known to you the power and **coming** [parousia] of our Lord Jesus Christ (the Messiah), but we were **eyewitnesses** of His majesty (grandeur, authority of sovereign power) (2 Peter 1:16 AMP).*

Peter here was saying that they were well equipped to preach the final coming *(parousia)* of Jesus because they "saw" the full revelation of it when Jesus revealed it to them, which was none other than at the Mount of Transfiguration experience. However, Revelation 1:7 says that the rest of the world will eventually witness Jesus as the reigning King of Majesty. It says *"...and every eye shall see Him, and they also which pierced Him: and all kindreds of the earth shall wail because of Him. Even so, Amen."* Eventually every eye will see His coming and this event has yet to take place!

Nonetheless, I will grant to those in Preterism that some events could have certainly pointed to the time of A.D. 70, but undoubtedly point more clearly to a future time of catastrophic events, not only for Jerusalem but for the entire world. There is no question that while Jesus was addressing His own disciples, He was also sending a resounding sound on to the present-day Church!

However, in the end my real problem with Preterism is that it denies the literal return of Jesus Christ. In the end, that alone makes the doctrine heretical.

> *Their teaching will spread like gangrene. Among them are Hymenaeus and Philetus, who have wandered away from the truth. They say that the resurrection has already taken place, and they destroy the faith of some* (2 Timothy 2:17-18 NIV).

The danger with it today is that people simply don't want Jesus Christ to appear in supreme majesty and hold them or this entire planet accountable. That is my bottom-line point. Today, people are becoming increasingly hungry for this type of theology because it requires little spiritual readiness. The basic impression preterists often leave is that personal judgment takes place at death, but somehow that's not a real concern either because the Lake of Fire mentioned in Revelation, according to them, isn't literal either. Instead, they believe it to be a reference to a garbage dump that existed when Jerusalem was being destroyed, again referring to A.D. 70.

Full Preterism places hardly any focus on spiritual readiness or even any real need to fear eternal punishment because, after all, in their minds the fire of hell is not eternal, but considered to be a past event! It gives a false sense of peace and safety based on the idea that "everything bad has already happened." In a self-help crazed world where few want to face any form of judgment in their future, this is a convenient system of belief and is gaining a resurgence of popularity.

PARTIAL PRETERISM AND DOMINIONISM

This is another end-time mindset, which comes across even more palatable and is receiving new attention especially among some Charismatic groups. It is the idea of Partial Preterism and Dominionism. Referred to as Postmillennialism in decades past, these doctrines present the general idea that most of the cataclysmic events of Revelation have already happened. They say the only event that has yet to take place is Jesus' return in full majesty, but that cannot happen until the Church is fully victorious. For that to happen, the Church must basically Christianize the entire world, in essence *"taking dominion"* in accordance with God's command to Adam in Genesis 1:28. They say that once this happens, the Church will present itself to Jesus as glorious, and at this point all the world's kingdoms will completely become the Lord's (see Eph. 5:27; Rev. 11:15). There is a partial truth to their line of thought, but many problems with it as doctrine. But this is often true of misguided doctrines.

Dominionists are very similar to partial preterists. They both believe that the most destructive judgments of Revelation already happened in A.D. 70. That is because these judgments combined with Church persecution would have to happen in the middle of what is supposed to be a glorious takeover by Christians. This wouldn't seem like the kind of "taking dominion" usually described by them. Conveniently, if the judgments have already happened, there is nothing left to occur except for the Church to go subdue the nations. It's all toned with a feeling of total conquering by the Church, and most of the language about believers being held accountable is left out. This mindset helps many Christians feel less edgy of a sudden appearance of Jesus who might find them unprepared or even sinning.

Realistically, a global takeover is something the Church has not been able to do throughout history. This is probably because Jesus never intended it. The concept, although it sounds lovely, just hasn't proven out. While global evangelism is moving at a record pace, governments, national leaders, and worldwide celebrities are still just as ungodly today as they were thousands of years ago. In fact, as I cited in Chapter One, the world has become much more anti-Christ than in previous decades. There is a growing distaste for godliness and Christianity, not only in America, but in the world. The Bible makes it clear in many passages of Scripture that persecution will be with the Church for as long as we are on this planet (see 2 Tim. 3:12). Therefore, if persecution will always be here, then so will the ungodly who do the persecuting!

I believe this is true, not because the Church isn't being successful, but because Jesus never called the Church to set up a natural Kingdom before His return. Jesus isn't trying to reform this world's system; He is going to wipe the slate clean. Jesus' Kingdom isn't going to be established because we win every soul on earth to Christ. We are fooling ourselves to believe that every single soul and government will eventually quit resisting Jesus Christ. This goes against countless Scriptures, and to believe it we would almost have to throw out the entire New Testament. The world that is determined to remain rebellious will eventually *have* to be judged. In the meantime, the Lord is giving us as much opportunity as possible to reach as many souls as we can (see 2 Pet. 3:9). In this way, we "take dominion" and expand the spiritual Kingdom of Jesus Christ until His return. In that effort, I believe we will be most victorious!

The Great Commission was not a call to reform the secular worldly systems. It is to reach souls for Christ and teach them how to receive the Lord in their hearts and tell them about His second coming. In fact, if we take a quick look at Matthew, we can see what Jesus meant.

Therefore go and make disciples of all nations, baptizing them in the name of the Father and of the Son and of the Holy Spirit, and teaching them to obey everything I have commanded you. And surely I am with you always, to the very end of the age (Matthew 28:19-20 NIV).

Dominionists use these verses to make a case that Christians are called to reform nations. Now I do believe that whole nations certainly *can* experience mass revival in such a way that even the government can be affected by it. I believe we should pray for nations and governments because the Bible teaches us to do so, providing a peaceable environment for us (see 2 Tim. 2:1-4).

However, historically entire nations coming to repentance under the umbrella of a specific government entity has by no means been the pattern and isn't what Jesus was advocating as an expected goal for the Church. The word "nations" in the verse above is the word *ethnos*. It essentially means "race, tribe, or foreign nation."[4] Now this certainly could include an entire country, but the idea here is not for us to expect a reform of the governing systems of those nations so they can now be considered "Christian." Instead, Jesus' message was that we are to make disciples and be sure to include *every race* of people in that ongoing effort.

This would be more in keeping with how the early apostles made disciples. They went from country to country preaching to people. We never see them make attempts to reform nations until they ultimately overcame the governing powers. Paul never tried to overcome the powers of Rome with his preaching endeavors. While many cities in their day experienced massive revivals and multitudes were saved, we simply don't see a pattern of entire countries or social groups all-inclusively bowing down to Christ. In fact, the Church grew exponentially in spite of the exact opposite. They brought souls to the

Lord in the midst of vehement persecution. It was not because everyone in those regions turned to the Lord.

Today, we see millions attend Christian crusades in the continent of Africa in spite of tyrannical national leaders. Many are saved in those nations and many are not. Some make legitimate, life-changing conversions, while others go back to their ungodliness. Biblically speaking there will always be the believing and the unbelieving in every town, city, and nation. If you look at the big picture of the Bible and the experiences gleaned from the early church, you have to agree this is true. Some of the Church's greatest successes are in communists nations where millions are coming to the Lord. This is happening all while the nation itself is utterly anti-Christ. I think lately, especially in America, we have to be careful we don't make an idol out of politics to the point where we think that revival or reform is only effective if the government gets behind it. I think Jesus' ministry and the early apostles proved that the greatest miracles will occur when the government and the masses are against it.

Can entire nations literally come to Christ? It is certainly probable, and I don't doubt by the end there will literally be "sheep," or Christian-leaning nations. But we have to remind ourselves that this world's systems will pass away. I simply don't see that the Bible makes the conversion of secular governments or entire nations an expected goal in order for the church to become totally victorious and usher in Jesus' millennial reign.

In fact, I am of the mind that Jesus will return based on two things which can be supported biblically. While I don't want to spend a great deal of time proving the point on the subject here, I do think we should touch on it slightly. First, there will come a point when the spirit of anti-Christ in this world will no longer tolerate Christianity. In fact, the Bible points to such intense days of persecution that it will be difficult for Christians to endure them. There will come a point when the Church will have done all it can do with the lawless environment on earth. Second, it will be followed by a time when the Jews' eyes will be opened and the remnant of Israel spoken of in Scripture will call upon Jesus as Messiah. At that point, according to God's covenant promise, Jesus will be obligated to stand again on the Mount of Olives and appear as Israel's glorious King!

When the world has walled off the influence of Christianity and in turn Israel calls Jesus Lord, the time will come when Jesus will clean house on earth in defense of both Israel and His Church. Then both will stand together as the unified olive tree spoken of in Romans 11:15-25.

While there are many Scriptures to support this, probably one of the most compelling Scriptures says:

> *Lest you be self-opinionated (wise in your own con-*
> *ceits), I do not want you to miss this hidden truth*
> *and mystery, brethren: a hardening (insensibility)*
> *has [temporarily] befallen a part of Israel [to last]*
> *until the full number of the ingathering of the Gen-*
> *tiles has come in* (Romans 11:25 AMP).

The Amplified Bible here uses the phrase *full number*. The King James uses *fullness*. In the Greek, the word is *pleroma* which basically means "completion."[5] In other words, there will come a point in time when the ingathering of the Gentiles will be completed or finished, but until that happens Israel's blinders will remain intact.

Some interpret this verse to say that the full number of Gentiles is only the certain count of Gentiles that God pre-destined or determined. But that doesn't make clear sense because Jesus told us to go and get as many as possible! For various reasons, I think that theory isn't as strong as the idea that the "number of completion" will occur whenever there are simply not a significant number of receptive souls still available to preach to simply because the growing worldly hold on people's minds will blind the masses to that extreme. We already see it happening. When that moment of completion so to speak occurs, only God will know the hour. When it does happen, however, Israel's eyes will do the reverse. They will be opened. Had they been opened prior to this, Jesus' return would have come before many Gentiles had the opportunity to hear the Gospel preached to them.

In the end, the doctrine of Dominionism places little focus on spiritual readiness. Sure, Christians are to "prepare" themselves for their finest hour, but in the Dominion doctrine there appears to be no time limit on the effort according to this teaching. Apparently, we can take as long as we want. That means if half the Body of Christ decides to backslide this year, we put off taking dominion until next year when everyone gets their act in order. In Dominionism, there is little mention of potential correction or even judgment for disobedient saints; they only talk of the victorious side of the Church. Yet, the Bible repeatedly mentions the need for saints to be ready for Christ's coming. Under Dominion theology, why would we have to bother worrying about it? All we need to do is watch the nations and see how close they are to conversion and get things in order then.

I think doctrines like this endanger believers and cause them to fall into a slumber mode. Sure, there are some who are laying their lives down to take dominion, but I struggle to believe this will be the effort of the Church on a large scale or the Bible wouldn't have needed to keep making repeated warnings in order to keep the fear of God underneath our backside.

Instead, the glorious Church will be those who are working every day to promote and stand for the Gospel in their sphere of influence as they keep a watchful eye on the actions of their own lives, ready and watchful for His glorious appearing that could occur at any moment (see 1 Tim. 6:14, 2 Tim. 4:8, Titus 2:13, Heb. 9:28, 1 John 2:28). His appearing is something we should prepare for every day, so that when the day arrives it doesn't catch us unprepared.

> *But you, brothers, are not in darkness so that this*
> *day should surprise you like a thief. You are all sons*
> *of the light and sons of the day. We do not belong to*
> *the night or to the darkness. So then, let us not be*
> *like others, who are asleep, but let us be alert and*
> *self-controlled* (1 Thessalonians 5:4-6 NIV).

A world that is increasingly desirous of "peace and safety" can be vulnerable to any idea that diminishes the need for spiritual readiness.

UNIVERSALISM

This doctrine has been denounced as heresy by the present-day Church, but once again is gaining audience because people want a Gospel that doesn't hold them accountable. They want self-help and happiness without paying a price for holiness and sacrifice. As I mentioned in Chapter Three, Universalism is the doctrine that basically teaches that all things will eventually be reconciled to God and that there is no literal hell in the form of eternal torment or judgment.

Years ago, my husband and I broke acquaintance with a group of pastors who decided to embrace this teaching. Most Christians today are still quite adamant against Universalism in its purest form. However, because the world is more willing than ever to receive things that don't require anything of them, I feel it is important to include it in the doctrines that ignore the need for spiritual readiness. I also feel it is important to mention it because some key ministers and leaders in the Charismatic movement have gone down the road of Universalism and lost their ministries. So this doctrine carries a deceptive and alluring quality for people who don't want to accept the idea that their actions will be called to accountability, potentially to the point of eternal punishment.

THE DOCTRINE OF ETERNAL SECURITY

This one is less common to Charismatics and more common among certain denominations and evangelicals. It basically teaches that once you are born again you cannot "lose" salvation regardless of your actions because grace is completely free. Proponents state that our works play no part in our salvation.

The problem is that many genuine Christians backslide and end up doing some deplorable things. While supporters of eternal security say that those people could have never been genuine Christians in the first place, they ignore Scriptures that give clear examples of genuine Christians who departed from the faith (see 1 Tim. 4:1). That means they started out on a legitimate journey of faith in Christ, but somewhere along the way lost their Christian focus.

Whether supporters of the doctrine want to believe it or not, there *are* people who genuinely have a salvation experience but later fall back into the ways of the world. The Bible constantly warns the believers of this potential pitfall and the fact that they might not be prepared to meet Jesus when He returns.

This doctrine seems to overlook the scriptural warnings for spiritual readiness and holy living needed in order to be prepared for Christ's return. These admonishing Scriptures were not written to the world; they were written to genuine believers. While advocates of eternal security will try to make a case to say that the doctrine doesn't give license for believers to sin or backslide, the reality is that many Christians who believe it aren't focused on the daily *need* for spiritual sobriety. Rather, sin or compromise, under this teaching, could easily be seen as an option that is automatically forgiven even if the person doesn't purposely repent. The Bible repeatedly warns believers against the danger of such behavior.

Again, this doctrine makes it difficult to promote the important need for living in a constant state of spiritual readiness for Christ's imminent return.

My motive here is to help Christians discern that there are countless doctrines resurfacing today that leave out the Bible's focus on spiritual readiness. They make it "too safe," and we need to be discerning in an hour when people are hungry for anything that will support the sinful side of who they are today and have little expectation for the accountability of their actions, lifestyle, and personal decisions.

NO DEMAND FOR REPENTANCE OR ACCOUNTABILITY

While there are certain doctrines that promote a sense of false peace about the future end times, there are also ideals that simply treat all confrontation and admonishing material as if it should somehow be unmentionable. Sin is less often being referred to as sin in the pulpits. It is now more palatable to refer to it as a dysfunction, problem, misfortune, or disability. Today there is an excusable reason for nearly every type of uncontrolled behavior. "The children act that way because their parents got divorced." "The wife acted that way because her husband did something wrong." Either they were born that way, couldn't help it, or it was someone else's fault.

Certainly, our personal experiences can play into the pattern of our behaviors. Habits we grew up with—good or bad, often learned from parents—usually form our way of life. Much of who we are is the result of a series of experiences and things passed down generationally. In many cases, from the time we were children we had little control over those in our lives who helped form us.

God understands this sad detriment to the human race that came through the curse of Adam. In fact, we often refer to it as generational curses and thank God these curses are destroyable in the power of Jesus' Name!

Yet again, we have to see another growing trend. The secular world has become overly sensitive to these dysfunctional issues in the lives of people. Psychological help is being made available to people of all ages at record levels. Massive programs are offered in schools and universities to fix the growing number of emotional dysfunctions. People everywhere are expressing increased understanding for people's problems. Of course, there is nothing wrong with wanting to help people.

However, now the trend of "compassion" is growing to where even preachers are less bold about calling bad behavior sin. We are expected to feel so sorry for people that we feel the pressure to almost excuse them. That is because confronting it as sin places the direct responsibility on the one who did the wrong, while a dysfunction or misfortune allows it to fall on someone else.

While Jesus deeply understands the pain and agony of people's lives, it doesn't diminish the need for repentance from sin. Hebrews says:

> *For we have not an High Priest which cannot be touched with the feeling of our infirmities; but was in all points tempted like as we are, yet without sin* (Hebrews 4:15).

Jesus could have made all the same excuses people make for their issues. There isn't anything on this planet that Jesus doesn't understand, but He still expects us to own up to our behaviors and call them sin. Why? Because refusing to do so diminishes your need for a Savior and His blood. After all, if you didn't do "wrong," you shouldn't be punished right? Not true, the fact is that we did do wrong. We have all sinned. Regardless of whatever bad habit, addiction, vice, or dysfunction, we need to be accountable for our own sin, even if the iniquity or curse was passed down from someone else.

We can't overlook the need for a person to repent just because we feel sorry about what they've gone through or because of where they came from.

This is becoming harder to expect today in a world of excuses. These excuses have crept into the Church. In addition, people today are enjoying the feeling of compassionate attention they receive from those who help them walk through their "issue." It makes them feel good about themselves, and there is nothing wrong with wanting to feel better. Where this trend has become a problem is that many are ignoring the important need to call sin, sin. Being accountable at that level is considered too harsh for some people.

Many don't want the pastor to shoot straight with them and tell them they need to get right with God and repent of their sins. With the help of modern-day self-help thinking, they are convinced that they have not legitimately done anything that deserves accountability. They just want to continue with the mindset that they have a valid reason for their issues. Then they feel that because those issues are "special" or unique, they can deal with it as they see fit. They want to address their behaviors in a way that makes them feel comfortable, not through straightforward accountability to Jesus or the boundaries of the Bible.

I am amazed today how many people don't want to hear a straightforward message from the pulpits. They run to pastors who always preach the encouraging messages mixed with humorous anecdotes. They want "bless me" preaching but never any "correct me" preaching. They want only prophetic words that make them happy, but never want them to contain an admonition. They don't want to hear anything that strikes the fear of God in their hearts or makes them measure their life against God's standards. They want all the preaching to stay away from doctrine that demands that they make changes that conform to the Kingdom of God.

They want God's love to replace His justice so they can go on through life happy as they are. Many churches are proud to advertise:

"Come as you are!" Sure, we want people to come to church no matter what condition their life is in because we have the answers to help them. But in order to help them, we can't let them think they can "come as they are" and then be allowed to stay that way. We have to preach a repentance Gospel that will demand a change of their entire life—a total conversion.

I would encourage you to discern any hint of this tendency in your own personal life. Are there things you avoid because you don't want to face what is inside? No, you don't have to beat yourself up or see yourself as a hopeless failure. That is by no means what Jesus' blood accomplished for you. What His blood did was allow you and me the wonderful ability to lay our sins and failures at the feet of Jesus, own up to them, and then leave them at the Cross. But to do that means we have to get real. We have to be real with ourselves the way David was when Nathan the prophet confronted him about adultery saying, *"Thou art the man"* (see 2 Sam. 12:7). David didn't respond to the confrontation by making excuses for himself. He responded by saying *"I have sinned against the Lord"* (2 Sam. 12: 13). I believe that is why God said David was a man after His heart and why Jesus Himself was from the lineage of David.

Don't let a "peace and safety" attitude allow you to cover sin and avoid facing up to wrong behaviors. Discern them and let the Lord deal with them. This is so important in this hour.

NO SACRIFICIAL REQUIREMENTS

In the mindset of all things being about peace and safety these days, people also want the Gospel to be convenient. They might like Jesus as long as He doesn't interfere too much in their pursuit of happiness. Sure, they might consider church attendance once in a while, but the requirements can't go beyond that because they might have to miss dancing lessons.

Now personally, the way my husband and I pastor our church, we try hard not to overload people with too many church functions. I think there is a fine balance we ministers have to consider with that. I do believe too many churches don't promote family togetherness enough, and I encourage families to spend time at home to make a stable family environment. People need to slow down so they can pray, read their Bible, and take care of their families. So I don't want you to get the impression that I am implying sacrifice for the Kingdom means being swamped to the point of the mental breakdown! As pastors, we want people to make sacrifices, not just be overly busy with unnecessary activities.

What I do want to address is the modern drop in church attendance overall and the fact the people are less willing to live a sacrificial Kingdom lifestyle. Much of the U.S. population is going to church less, but with all of the distractions today, church attendance is being challenged more than ever, even in our Spirit-filled congregations.

Today in many regions, little league is now played on Sunday, so people miss church if their kids play baseball. More jobs are demanding employees work Sundays. Some have two jobs in order to make ends meet. Even in a world of modern conveniences, people seem to have less time for everything, so church attendance often drops as a priority.

It seems that in order to keep up with everything and get to all the things that demand time, people need to make cuts somewhere. In the effort to remain stress-free, people are spending more time on long vacations, going to the gym, or taking up expensive and time-consuming hobbies. Usually, what gets reduced in people's schedule is time for the Kingdom of God.

We have to be honest. Bible reading can take five minutes but a tennis tournament five hours. Prayer can be 20 minutes, but shopping two or three hours. More people want church to last an hour, but they will take all day for some form of R and R.

Sure, the Lord wants us to relax, but if we aren't careful our relax mode can turn into an effort to avoid as many things as possible that make us feel like we have more work to do. Then, eventually we find ourselves among the crowds of people who want the Gospel as long as it remains convenient. Reality is that spreading the Gospel is work. It requires sacrifices, and sometimes the Gospel of the Kingdom will make you feel uncomfortable. We cannot avoid it.

Dedication to the Gospel can land you in the middle of controversy, and many people today just don't want to deal with it. They want life to be nice! I often wonder what would happen if we all started preaching the Gospel the way the early church apostles did. I am sure there would be a great deal more occurrences of rubbing people's fur the wrong way! The unbelieving Jews in Thessalonica said this of them in Acts 17:6: *"These that have turned the world upside down are come...."* They weren't giving them a compliment. The New Living Translation says, *"...have caused trouble all over the world...and now they are here disturbing our city, too."*

You see, their preaching made waves everywhere they went. Nearly every time they opened their mouths there was an uproar!

Yes, we still have Christian people who are willingly making waves against certain forms of legislation that go against our Christian values, but what would happen if the average Christian truly made the kind of waves the early church did, just because they were seriously dedicated? What would happen if people really put their lives on the line for the Word of God?

The apostle Paul said of Aquila and Priscilla, *"Who have for my life laid down their own necks: unto whom not only I give thanks, but also all the churches of the Gentiles"* (Rom. 16:4). They weren't afraid to put their necks on the line for the Gospel. That means they made sacrifices.

In a day and age of people wanting all things "good," we have to make sure we keep Kingdom business as a top priority because sometimes it will stir up opposition. That alone may make you want to drift toward the trap of convenient Christianity. The Kingdom requires sacrifices.

Over the years, some people who initially started coming to our church would often say thing like, "Pastor, we really like this church, but just so you know, we were overly busy in our last church and we need a break! So we don't plan to get too involved or come to every service." I can appreciate when people have gotten exhausted, but the Kingdom today in our lives still requires sacrifice and commitment. That is a foundational basic for being a legitimate Christian. There just isn't room for the safe and comfortable lifestyle that people want today. Past commitment and sacrifice don't cut it. What are we doing today, not just as a church attendee, but as a Kingdom believer who wants nothing more than to see souls saved and lives changed by the power of God?

As we close this chapter, I want to encourage you to exercise discernment when the "peace and safety" tendency may be trying to take hold of you. Whether it be a subtle doctrine, complacent lifestyle, or things you just don't want to deal with, ask the Holy Spirit to keep the fire of God burning hot in your heart.

Sure, the Lord may inconvenience you and He may have to admonish you sometimes. He may ask you to evaluate the future and your own road to eternity. He may ask you to give up things. Be willing to exercise discernment, confront yourself, and make the commitments needed. Then when the "peace and safety" trend continues down the road of comfortable ideals and lifestyles, you will be making ground and increasing in the power of God!

ENDNOTES

1. SearchGodsWord.org, "Eido," Bible Study Resources from HeartLight.org, Definition, http://www.searchgodsword.org/lex/grk/view.cgi?number=1492 (accessed August 20, 2010).

2. SearchGodsWord.org, "Erchomai," Bible Study Resources from HeartLight.org, Definition, http://www.searchgodsword.org/lex/grk/view.cgi?number=2064 (accessed July 11, 2010).

3. SearchGodsWord.org, "Parousia," Bible Study Resources from HeartLight.org, Definition, http://www.searchgodsword.org/lex/grk/view.cgi?number=3952 (accessed August 20, 2010).

4. Church of the Great God, "Ethnos," Greek/Hebrew Definitions, Strong's #1484, http://www.bibletools.org/index.cfm/fuseaction/Lexicon.show/ID/G1484/ethnos.htm (accessed July 11, 2010).

5. SearchGodsWord.org, "Pleroma," Bible Study Resources from HeartLight.org, Definition, http://www.searchgodsword.org/lex/grk/view.cgi?number=4138 (accessed July 11, 2010).

Chapter Seven

DISCERNING THE SEEKER-FRIENDLY MOVEMENT AND THE NEW "GOSPEL" OF TOLERANCE

And they shall teach My people the
difference between the holy and profane,
and cause them to discern between the
unclean and the clean (Ezekiel 44:23).

"I am shortening up my sermons and changing my entire format in order to be more relevant," a pastor friend of ours reported. "I feel that if I want to grow my church, I have to relate to the culture. Believe me, I have learned the hard way!" he said.

When we started our church, truthfully our vision could just about be summed up in one sentence. It was: *Preach the uncompromising Word and demonstrate the power of God.* In the early years, we were hungry to see God raise up a church that had the presence of God. We started the church from scratch in 1997 with a small handful of people, a few chairs (that someone donated), and a small folding table for a pulpit. We rented a small retail space totaling 3,800 oddly-shaped square feet. We had one storeroom-like space for kids' Sunday school and another small room we used as the nursery. There were two single restrooms and one closet that became our office. We nicknamed it the "clo-ffice." Believe it or not, we counseled people in that clo-ffice!

The place had nasty blue shag carpet. We painted the walls "prison green" with some paint someone got free at work. For seating, we had a mix of brown folding chairs and some bright orange pews that were donated from another church. When we got those pews, however, they didn't have any legs, so a carpenter in our church offered to make some. What we didn't account for was that the pews were designed for an auditorium with a sloped floor. So the newly-added legs forced the seats to sit at an odd angle so everyone sat slightly perched forward. But it worked. We made the place as perfect as we could.

From these most humble beginnings we just wanted to see people raised up who loved the Word of God and wanted to see the Lord move in signs, wonders, and miracles.

We had been in other various forms of ministry nearly all of our adult life, but this would have been the first time as senior pastors and first time planting a church. Wanting to be the best pastors we knew how to be, we always looked for input from other pastor friends.

That was when our friend told us what he was doing in his church. He decided he needed to make a move so his church would be more interesting to would-be attendees and help its growth.

Well, we had been experiencing a little growth ourselves at the time, but nothing exponential. Every pastor who starts a church is probably convinced that his newly-formed church is special and will grow to 1,000 members by the end of the year! We had faith, you know!

Yes, our church grew, but only little by little. By 1999, we moved to another space in the shopping center, not because we gloriously grew out of our current one, but because the neighboring business complained to the landlords about our drums being too loud on Sunday morning! The property manager at the time told us if we didn't quiet down we would have to leave. We explained to them that as a church it was just necessary to have music! I mean, what is a Spirit-filled anointed church with no music? So we told them we would lower the volume a little and put pillows in the drums, and he said that might be OK. Well, it wasn't. The neighbors complained again.

Before we knew it, the landlord told us we would have to move out and that he was going to lock the door. Our church was only about 18 months old by then, and we didn't know what to do. The manager gave us one option: to take a larger space in the same center of about 8,000 square feet. It was only a few doors down, so it seemed reasonable. The problem was it was going to cost us a whopping 300 dollars more a month and the place was a wreck! That seemed like an astronomical number back then, plus the cost of having to fix up the place. Wow! To even make it work as a church, the space would almost have to be gutted.

Nevertheless, we went for it because we had no other options. People donated time, money, and contracting labor, and before we knew it, we had a nice new facility! It had a real sanctuary, much bigger than our previous one. It had four separate classrooms and three real offices! Amazingly, with a little effort, we even got a loan for some new church chairs. The place looked incredible! We were sure this would interest people in coming to our church.

However, since the auditorium was bigger now, we would walk out on Sunday and the place looked so empty. Each week passed—still not full. Another week and another. We preached every Sunday the uncompromised Word of God, prayed for the sick, prophesied to people, and ministered in the anointing. Surely, people were hungry for the power of God, right?

That is when our friend told us of the new steps he was taking to grow his church. I remember us thinking to ourselves, "Well, that really isn't for us," but the truth is when your church remains a handful of members you begin to wonder what you aren't doing right.

In addition to that, for a season it seemed like nearly every visitor we had never came back. In fact, not only would they not come back, they would sit through the services with their arms folded and scowls on their faces. Some walked out! We tried everything. We made sure they were given a visitor packet and greeters were friendly at the door. We made sure the place was perfectly clean and ushers were all in place. The church was in perfect order from top to bottom, and we even smiled at people! We couldn't figure it out.

Now, realize in the middle of this we did have some growth. Many wonderful people came and got committed to the church. But again—little by little. While a few visitors would stay, most would leave.

When you have done all you know as a pastor, this is when you start to think, *Maybe it's me; maybe people don't like the preaching, the ministry, or the music. Maybe I should change some things and give people what they want and they will come back to church.* Then, in the middle of not experiencing a ton of growth, some people we already did have left the church!

I kid you not, during that same season we ran into not only one pastor, but many others who told us they were reformatting their concept of church in order to encourage growth. They were making it more casual and preaching only things that might feel less threatening to a visitor. They were serving cookies, doing skits, and offering to get people out by a certain time. They told us, "You really should consider making some changes." They encouraged us not to use a Sunday morning to pray for the sick and that we might want to consider avoiding any speaking in tongues during that time, too. They would say, "You know, the gifts of the Spirit might scare some people."

We thought, "Really? We thought everyone wants to experience the power of God." It worked on our minds quite a few times.

Now, I will pause to say that there are some valid reasons people don't stay in some of our Charismatic churches. Sometimes an overall lack of excellence, disorderly services, no good planning, and unnecessary extremes *do* frighten newcomers. I have been in services where things were unduly wild and sometimes just sloppy. So there is excellence needed in how we handle things if we do want to have a strong anointing in our lives and if we want to grow our churches.

However, what worked on us was that we were feeling the pressure to hide the Holy Spirit altogether and preach diluted content. For a period of time in our church, we were really caught in the middle.

Then one night my husband went to the church to pray. He talked to God about it, and something in him rose up and he kicked one of the auditorium chairs and said, "Lord, I will not kiss up to dead religion!"

Well, God took him up on the offer. One Sunday following, still trying to find our way on what was considered too radical or too reserved for a Spirit-filled church, something happened. My husband finished his sermon and called people to the front for prayer. There were visitors there that day, but all I remember is that people in the line started manifesting demons! Some people fell on the floor. Some screamed. I think one person threw up. As I reached my hand out to pray for one lady, I saw a bat-like creature fly off her chest! It was a demon. The place was berserk all in front of the visitors, and we didn't even try to start anything. We were trying so hard to present a pleasing environment for visitors!

That day we learned something. People *do* want the power of God. They want an uncompromised Gospel that will tell them the truth and set them free. They want genuine healing, deliverance, and the presence of the Holy Spirit. We realized that people know that skits and cookies, while fun and enjoyable sometimes, ultimately won't set you free!

Since that time, my husband and I have decided we would rather preach a straightforward message and demonstrate the power of God. Once we made that decision, our church began to grow into a stronger church. From 2001 to 2008, we expanded the facility five more times and rebuilt the entire auditorium, and in 2009 we added a second Sunday morning service to accommodate the people. At the time of this writing, we are exploring options to expand again.

Interestingly, the pastors who told us to become more relevant don't have their churches today. They quit and went looking for something else because they weren't succeeding. One pastor quit the ministry altogether.

I've realized that even in a society that wants all things nice and comfortable, there are still people who are hungry and desperate for an honest message coupled with the demonstrations of God. These desperate people are out there! We can't be coaxed into giving these a diluted version because of others who reject truthful sermons that are combined with the power of the Spirit. Paul said:

> *And my speech and my preaching was not with enticing words of man's wisdom, but in demonstration of the Spirit and of power* (1 Corinthians 2:4).

Paul didn't *replace* the anointing with a skit or message that was sure to please the ears of his listeners. He didn't consume himself with making sure everyone was at ease with what he had to say. Instead, we know from Paul that he came preaching a straightforward, uncompromising Gospel. And he did so coupled together with the demonstrations of the power of God.

REACHING THE CULTURE OR RELATING TO THEM?

There is a recent trend of pastors, churches, and even believers who feel it's important to make Christianity appear as something the world can relate to. The concept is crossing into nearly all streams and camps, and we need to discern it. It isn't just limited to denominations or evangelicals, but has filtered into many Charismatic churches. We've commonly referred to this concept as the *seeker-friendly* or *user-friendly* type of ministry. The premise of it states that if we can relate to the culture and give them things they are familiar with and are unthreatened by, then we have a better chance of reaching them.

The movement places the predominant focus on creating a positive experience. They believe that, because this is what everyone in the world is looking for, we need to provide it for them. Therefore, the goal is to present Christianity as people's next positive experience. They feel that once people experience it this way it will dispel their previous negative mindsets. If they can get people to see that Christianity could easily fit their normal lives without feeling too out of the ordinary, then they think people might accept it.

The seeker-friendly idea also believes that if we will provide more of what people in the world are interested in, we will be better equipped to reach them. If people are interested in sports, then we feel we should provide ample sports related activities. If we get the idea that the latest interest is support groups, then that is what we start. Since we know the current generation is a media generation, we work hard to provide plenty of visual aids, dramas, and video.

Initially, this all seems like a very good and reasonable line of thinking, but as discerning believers we should take the time to filter through it. Sometimes what looks like the best idea in the world may be nothing more than adding water to gasoline. It's simply not going to get you where you really want to go.

There is certainly nothing wrong with creating avenues of interest and providing things that aid us in ministry, such as drama or videos. These can all help make our churches more well-rounded. Churches as well as individual believers should work to help people see how fulfilling the Christian life is.

Jesus Himself related to people on their level and showed them His love. He talked to sinners and listeners about subjects that related to their lives. He offered to have dinner with Zacchaeus the tax collector. He passed out food to people who came to hear Him preach. He rescued the abused woman caught in adultery. These humanitarian and friendly efforts are important aspects to presenting the Gospel.

However, here is where we have often gotten off-course. We have made these things the *focus* of our outreach, while we have made the all-important task of clearly presenting the Word of God secondary. Many times, the actual message is being overshadowed by all the frills and trimmings.

But here is an even bigger problem. More and more commonly, certain parts of the Word of God are being deliberately left out or creatively reworded in order not to scare or offend people. We no longer want to mention the word "satan" or "demons." We would rather say "problem." We don't want to call hell a place of torment and eternal punishment; we only want to call it a place of separation from God. For those who presently aren't interested in God, that probably sounds like a good deal! Some are even removing all or most mentions of the word "blood" in reference to the blood of Jesus from their tenants because it is considered too abrasive.

Many Charismatics have added an additional dimension to toning down their message. They are also choosing to minimize any Spirit-filled expressions that visitors might not be familiar or comfortable with. They don't want any speaking in tongues or anyone falling under the power of the Spirit on a Sunday morning. Slowly the church experience throughout the Body of Christ is beginning to feel like nothing more than an uplifting social gathering that is not much different than a country club or YMCA membership.

We can't just relate to the culture through familiar means; we also need to reach them with the honest Kingdom message.

Reaching someone by definition means that you help get them to a new destination, while *relating* to them means that you look for a way to form a common relationship. Now right there, proponents of the seeker-friendly concept will say, "Yes, but if you look for a common ground, then you will be better able to reach them." There is some truth to that, and we already saw how Jesus even did some of those things.

I will reiterate that I am certainly of the mind that we can and should, when appropriate, use many of these common-ground methods to aid our ministry endeavors. There is nothing wrong with promoting a drama, showing a video, or handing out mints. I have no problem with keeping services shorter and more to the point as long as they create a place for the anointing. We can even offer donuts and coffee in the reception area after service. Yet there are times you need to eliminate the dramas and presentations and just let the Word of God speak for itself.

Reaching someone means you take them from where they are to where you are. Once they come into our churches, there will finally come a point where there isn't always a non-offensive way to bring them up to the Kingdom level where we are. The Gospel message and the boundaries defined in the Bible may offend. At that point in time, there may be no common ground in between.

After the "Have a cookie in a casual atmosphere!" advertisement gets them in the door, we are required to present the same Word Jesus preached. We can't get so overly excited once people come to the church that we feel the need to tone down Bible truths or demonstrations of the

Spirit so they'll stay. That is where the common ground ends and the unwilling are separated from the willing. Sometimes when people are faced with their own spiritual condition, shown the requirements of true Christianity, or even exposed to the anointing, they may not respond positively. Suddenly, the experience in their minds isn't so positive!

Jesus didn't preach a common-ground message, He preached the Kingdom in plain terms. Ultimately, His message was pretty hard hitting. His message was meant to reach them and bring them into the Kingdom. He started His ministry with, *"Repent, for the kingdom of heaven is at hand"* (Matt. 4:17). He preached a Gospel that commanded self-crucifixion and sacrifice. It was during the Sermon on the Mount before the general public where Jesus preached, *"Narrow is the gate and difficult is the way which leads to life, and there are few who find it"* (Matt. 7:14 NKJV). It was in front of a large congregation of people from all walks of life that He said, *"Why call ye Me, Lord, Lord, and do not the things which I say?"* (Luke 6:46).

The message Jesus preached was the Gospel of the Kingdom. The Kingdom message He came to deliver was *God's government and God's way of doing things.* The Kingdom message of His ministry always included three basic ingredients:

1. *Repentance*—The expectation of repentance was to admit sin, followed up by a total change of lifestyle patterned after God's commandments (see Matt. 4:17).

2. *Teaching/Preaching*—Jesus preached the benefits of the Kingdom as well as the sacrificial principles and boundaries necessary for living in the Kingdom (see Matt. 4:23).

3. *Demonstrations of Power*—His Kingdom message was followed up with the supernatural.

> There was healing, deliverance, spiritual
> impartations, signs, and wonders (see Matt.
> 4:23-25).

Sure, Jesus related to people on natural human levels, but actually those were rarely the methods He used to get them to hear Him. Relating to them through some of the natural methods was a very small fraction of how He touched lives. Instead, Jesus related the Kingdom to them by offering healing, signs, and wonders. He cast out devils and performed creative miracles. These were the actual drawing cards for the crowds, and the Bible records it was why they followed Him! He didn't give out candy, He healed the diseased! They listened to His hard-hitting Kingdom message because His supernatural manifestations were setting them free.

Then He commanded repentance, and it wasn't in such soft terms that listeners could have mistaken it for a casual suggestion. Unfortunately, much modern-day preaching sounds like good ideas or suggestions.

This is where we have to trust the *power* of the Gospel. Always making sure we are doing "all the right things" to make people's church experience a positive one pressures us to diminish the anointing. Suddenly, we aren't trusting that the living power of God's Word presented in raw form has the power to move them or prick their hearts. Countless Bible examples show that when the Word was plainly preached or miracles were in manifestation there were always two results. Either people received it gladly or they rejected it. It separated and brought clarity between the rebellious and the hungry.

Relating to people or being relevant must be secondary to our message. If the relevant method diminishes the message it must take a back seat or in some cases be thrown out altogether. The problem with the seeker-friendly trend is that most pastors are not only using dramas, casual dress, and free snacks, they are also toning down the Word of God and His tangible presence. With some methods, churches are becoming *so* relevant they have crossed the line into accepting worldly compromise.

RESULTS OF A SEEKER-FRIENDLY APPROACH

So we have to ask ourselves what kind of Christians are being developed through a seeker-friendly approach. Does it raise up people with a "positive" take on Christianity or create genuine Christians with the stamina to lay their lives down for Jesus? The whole term *seeker-friendly* denotes the idea that it's all about making a welcoming environment that gives those who are "seeking" what they would expect to experience. It isn't as much about expecting them to adjust to what God requires. To accomplish this, the approach must usually include a toned-down message meant to keep people's experience feeling positive.

This kind of effort keeps us subjected to the opinions of the people because we always have to keep figuring out what they want next. From there we find our ministry plans and programs are all the result of popular demand and not what the Lord directs.

Always creating the environment that gives people what they want rather than what they need won't grow them into mature Christians. There is a vast difference between a mature *Christian* and a mature *person*. There are many people in the world who don't serve the Lord that are mature, quality people. They have good jobs, they are involved in community and humanitarian efforts, and they have a decent family life. For the most part, they do all the right things to create a stable lifestyle. However, they don't know the first thing about the requirements for living in the Kingdom.

These may not have Kingdom standards about certain secular activities. They think it's OK to spend limited time in the casinos or attend happy hour with co-workers. They think certain movies are fine or that it's OK to listen to secular rock and roll. They think certain kinds of apparel are fine. That is because they don't have a Kingdom perspective.

Many immature or marginal Christians think along these lines right along with these secular people who appear to lead decent lives. That is why we need honest pastors and preachers. These leaders are called to define the difference between the Kingdom of God and the secular world in a clear manner that doesn't come across like a non-threatening suggestion.

> *And they shall teach My people the difference between*
> *the holy and profane, and cause them to discern*
> *between the unclean and the clean* (Ezekiel 44:23).

If we rarely ever preach a direct Gospel that commands righteousness, then how will people know what activities and lifestyles are sinful by God's standards? We have to teach people to separate their lifestyles from the world (see 2 Cor. 6:17).

The early church leaders preached a Word that separated the Kingdom of God from the world. It offended, created division, and caused riots. They clarified what was sin and what wasn't. They weren't afraid to address disorderly behavior in the church or confront the gainsayers.

Now, they didn't deliberately try to make this happen. They didn't attack anyone with clubs or walk around with picket signs. They didn't go around with their nose in the air looking down on sinners. They just preached the truth, and the Word of God divided. It separated those who were in the flesh and those who were of the Spirit just by being spoken and demonstrated (see Heb. 4:12).

We can't spend so much time trying to make the world love us until we end up with nothing to offer. Many Christians and pastors today are doing everything they can to create a version of Christianity that the world can accept and tolerate. Jesus said, *"Woe unto you, when all men shall speak well of you!"* (Luke 6:26).

That doesn't sound to me like we are to present a Gospel that everyone will speak about positively. I understand showing community kindness, manners, and love. Jesus did those things, but He also had to draw a line of separation.

These days, no one wants to appear as a separatist. We all want to blend together until it sounds like another rendition of the song, "We Are the World."

I believe this is a terrible danger. It doesn't build Kingdom people; it builds a generation of professing Christians that are casual and carnal. We end up with people that fit very well into the world's ideals. You can hardly tell the difference between them and the others. Because they came to Christianity based on what they wanted and on their own terms, they will only stay involved with it as long as their terms are honored. When God's terms demand something from them that they don't want to relinquish, they leave.

Can the seeker-friendly approach create Kingdom believers? I struggle to believe so. Mature Christians understand the Bible and follow its commands. They face the reality of eternity and they know that Christianity requires a heavy price. They are willing to be inconvenienced and lay their lives down for the Lord.

As a pastor, I would rather know that I have strong believers in my church who will remain radical Christians when the going gets tough. I don't want to feel I have a group of people who are there to fulfill their own expectations of church and are nowhere around when the storms blow against the Body of Christ.

DISCERNING THE NEW GOSPEL OF TOLERANCE

It used to be that people always wanted to accuse Christians of being hypocritical. The new word of late that comes against the church is not so much the word "hypocrite," but now it's the word "intolerant." Sure, Christians still get accused of being hypocrites, but now it seems the world appreciates it when we show a little hypocrisy and fit in with them somewhat. This way they can reason that it's OK to call yourself a Christian and keep a few vices.

Recently there is a new cry from the world that is demanding that Christians loosen up a little and expand their views. They feel that if Christians were really loving, they would "love and accept" people who have a different views or beliefs than they do. Anyone who doesn't is considered *intolerant*.

People think because pastors don't want to hire homosexuals that they are intolerant. If you speak up against couples living together who aren't married you are narrow-minded or intolerant. If you say that "without Christ you will suffer eternal punishment," you are intolerant and made to look like a religious fanatic. When Christian leaders say that natural disasters and upheaval in certain parts of the world may have some connection to pagan worship, they are classified as heartless and judgmental. Christians who refuse to find common ground with non-Christian religions are considered bigots and, yes, *intolerant*. Yet the apostle Paul was fearless to stand upon Mars' Hill and call their paganism into question and declare the command of repentance! (See Acts 17:22-24,30.)

The new expectation for the church is that we show love and tolerance for all religions and lifestyles, and the church has slowly begun to take it to heart. The devil is using this demand from the world to intimidate the church. The last thing most honest believers want to be considered as is unloving. After all, a lack of love goes against everything Christianity is about, and we don't want the very world we are trying to reach to perceive us as unloving. In an effort not to appear unloving, judgmental, or intolerant, many Christians and Christian groups are coming up with new techniques to prove otherwise.

Some are trying to dress more casual and trendy so people from the world will think we are simply "one of them." Others are changing their tenants of faith to use language that is more all-inclusive. There are pastors who are holding luncheons or gatherings that extend fellowship to leaders of other world religions and make a point to say, "We are getting together on all the things we can agree on and leaving out what we can't." However, in order to avoid a firestorm of controversy, many church leaders have avoided speaking up on what *can't* be agreed on, and the issues important to preaching the Gospel are being lost. No one anymore wants to use terms like *sin, abomination, immoral,* or *wrong* to describe any of the things embraced by the non-Christian community that go against the Bible. The problem is we aren't always even making these terms clear to our own Christian listeners for fear it may fall onto the wrong ears or be misunderstood. That is because of the fear that any form of direct disagreement on the part of the Christian community comes under the accusation of being intolerant and unloving. Christians want to preach to the world a "new" gospel, one that proves how loving and tolerant Christians are. It's the new gospel of tolerance.

The devil is cleverly selling the church the concept that to be good Christians we have to "love everybody" to the point that it requires us to minimize the appearance of any clear standards or beliefs.

A NEW ERA OF PERSECUTION

We really can't find a way to say it softly, but as the last days continue the world is growing less tolerant of the true Bible representation of the Church. There is no real way to make the Gospel more palatable. We simply have to accept that we won't be able to fit in if we are going to maintain the purity of the Gospel message. There is a great deal of Scripture about persecution of the Church. By acknowledging what the Bible says about it, we become less afraid to be discerning and vocal about what we believe because we won't let fear of persecution silence our voice.

It's good to have some persecution awareness. However, I am not saying that persecution awareness means you need to dig a bomb shelter, store food, and cancel your OnStar subscription in order to hide from government persecution. All these things are fear-motivated, and we never find the early church involved in this type of activity. Some people have become end-time prophecy junkies who live for nothing more than the next gimmick that will save them from the doom of the mark of the beast! This is not true persecution awareness at all.

What I want to address here is we Christians who have become so dull in our spiritual insight that we have lapsed into an almost peaceable relationship with worldliness. Some have found a tolerant and happy medium with the world just enough so that they see little threat for any persecution at all. That is *not* where God wants us to be, because the Bible says:

> *Yea, and all that will live godly in Christ Jesus shall suffer persecution. But evil men and seducers shall wax worse and worse, deceiving, and being deceived* (2 Timothy 3:12-13).

Persecution will be a part of the last days, and it *will grow!*

Of course, historically we have many examples of the persecuted Church clear back to the days of the Bible as well as comprehensive collections of stories in writings such as *Fox's Book of Martyrs*. However, it seems we have entered a new era of persecution—one that is steadily becoming global.

It seems that, more than ever, there is a growing global distaste and intolerance for Christianity. Nations are joining in a resounding sound that is increasingly anti-Christian or at least less Christian. The

United States once stood as the light for Christian ideals and principles among the other nations. Now it seems our nation is working harder to fit in with the more secular nations.

Most of us know that our nation was founded upon Christian principles. They are written and carved across the walls of our Senate and Congress. Certainly, many Americans still have Christian ideals within their root beliefs. Yet truthfully, Christian ideals are gradually growing dimmer in America as well as in other free nations. As we have been discussing, pure Christianity is not becoming more popular these days.

Prophetically, the new era of persecution that I see on the horizon is one where the world across the board is narrowing its receptivity of Christians at a record pace, making it probable that true biblical Christianity will become the new racial divide, with remnant believers being considered the real bigots of this age. It isn't hard to see that the world doesn't like our standard for righteousness, citing that if Christians really had love in their hearts they should accept and allow the views of special interest groups, homosexuals, humanists, atheists, multiple world religions, and liberal idealists. A Christian who doesn't accept these might easily be considered a bigot with no modern sense of tolerance. And of course, "those without tolerance" need to be dealt with.

We are living in a new world of "liberality for all." But the funny thing is that Christian liberties are the one growing source of tension as people increasingly feel that Christian expression should not be allowed in public forums.

We who live in free nations such as the United States shouldn't think that we will avoid persecution. I am not saying that in our lifetime, here in our own nation, we should immediately expect to join the ranks of martyrs who've spilled their blood. But if we are going to be discerning Christians who reject certain worldly ideals, we have to expect that persecution is imminent.

No longer in the United States can we just expect persecution to arise through governmental legislation alone, such as in cases of prayer being removed from school. It is increasing through a growing era of secularism in the heart of common society. There is a growing mindset of secular godlessness that affects our kids on the playground, teens at school, and us in our workplaces. We are looking at a generation today that is growing up without God altogether.

Not too long ago, I saw a bumper sticker that alarmed me. It pictured an American Flag in the shape of a heart, and next to it were the words, "Godless American." This attitude is growing rapidly among young Americans today, and it is becoming more powerful in its influence.

God is less a part of people's homes, and as a result more people are starting to deliberately resist the truth. Romans 1:25 says, *"Who changed the truth of God into a lie...."* This means they deliberately chose to trade the truth they knew in their hearts and accept lies that promote personal pleasure. Now people are looking to find new and creative ways to push the Lord out of society. The result is increased persecution against those who brightly shine the light of Jesus.

Some methods of persecution may be subtle. It may be a small group of co-workers who find your type of Christianity imposing. Even though they don't say it directly, they act funny about you reading Christian material in the break room during lunch. So they look for ways to make your job experience a challenge by purposely discussing crude things in your hearing, or maybe they complain about your performance to the boss or turn other employees against you.

If the pressure gets intense enough, some Christians will hide their light for fear of losing a promotion. In some cases, they must decide about their future on that job and now how to provide for their family.

Other scenarios are more obvious and intense but come in creative packages as well. In recent years, we have seen a growing number of court cases against Christian values, workers, teachers, and students litigating on the issue of separation of church and state. It is amazing how many cases are decided in favor of the secular view. The secular mindset in the world is indeed growing and becoming more commonplace as the Bible prophesied it would.

Look at Second Timothy. It says, *"This know also, that in the last days perilous times shall come"* (2 Tim. 3:1). This means the day we are living will be a dangerous time. Don't let your guard down regarding the ways of this world. To further this understanding, look also at the following verses. Here is a list of the types of people that will join the bandwagon against Christians and their standards in the last days. Second Timothy 3:2-5 says we will find:

- *Lovers of self*—Those who are dedicated to their own needs and comforts.

- *Covetous people*—These are never satisfied with what they already have; they love money and material things.

- *People who love to boast*—People who love to talk about themselves; braggers.

- *People full of pride*—People who emphasize self-importance over others.

- *Blasphemers*—These curse, swear, and blame God.

- *Disobedient to parents*—These have no honor to parents or proper authority.

- *Unthankful*—These are not grateful for the good things they've received.

- *Unholy*—People who fit in well with sin and dirty behavior.

- *Without natural affection*—Those who lack reasonable human kindness; hard-hearted people who turn a deaf ear to hurting people.

- *Trucebreakers*—People who are ruthless, pitiless, and show no mercy in their case; aggressive; abusive.

- *False accusers*—Literally means "of satan" (*diabolos*); those who accuse the righteous and righteous causes.

- *Incontinent*—People who lack self-control for sensual pleasure; addicts.

- *Fierce*—Ones who have rash outbursts of anger and rage; savage behavior.

- *Despisers of those that are good*—People who hate and resist righteousness and are hostile toward moral virtues.

- *Traitors*—Those who betray their friends for personal gain.

- *Heady*—People who respond without thinking; rash.

- *High-minded*—Those who think they have everything with little true substance; they blow a lot of smoke.

- *Lovers of pleasures more than lovers of God*—Ones who cannot get enough of their own desires for comfort, well-being, excesses, and luxury.

- *People with a form of godliness, but denying God's power*—Those who pretend to be Christians but want nothing to do with a real life change from God's power.

These kinds of people will be readily available in this hour to propagate the devil's lies and make anyone who wants to stand for the unadulterated Word feel like a fanatic with an intolerant point of view. Paul finishes by saying, *"...from such turn away"* (2 Tim. 3:5). In other words, don't try to make them accept you, and make sure that you don't become deceived into joining up with them.

As believers who carry a pure form of biblical discernment, we need to be careful that the seeker-friendly or "worldly-friendly" ideas aren't stealing our message and causing us to blend in. It's time to stand out and be separate. Those who truly desire the Kingdom of God will hear our voice and come to the sound of our message!

Chapter Eight

HOW TO DISCERN A GOOD CHURCH AND PASTOR

And I will give you pastors according to Mine heart, which shall feed you with knowledge and understanding (Jeremiah 3:15).

Having explored many of the needed ingredients for sharp discernment, as well as some of the modern-day issues that we need to discern, it's important to take some time discussing church leadership and the role of church in our lives. Believers today need to have a right foundation for discerning the character traits of good pastors or ministers from the bad. They also need to discern the important need for having a good church; otherwise, the devil could easily trick them into not prioritizing these things because of misunderstandings or misguided ideas. A lack of discernment surrounding these issues has knocked many believers out of their race or gotten them off course.

Unfortunately, because many have never taken the time to examine the biblical character traits that should be present in a good leader, they have sometimes mishandled them. On one hand, some good-hearted Christians have gotten entangled with leaders who abused their position, while others have erroneously accused good pastors of abuse and control. Often the second group made accusations out of ignorance or because of an offence over a personal issue the pastor held them accountable for.

As we discussed previously, there are practical skills for sharp discernment that will work in any circumstance. Let's recap them briefly, so they are fresh in our minds as we examine this subject.

1. *Recognize the times.* Keeping a strong sense of awareness about the dangers, deceptions. and signs of the last days keeps you watchful.

2. *Discern yourself.* A good and discerning Christian isn't afraid to put themselves in check. They aren't always pointing the finger of discernment at other things or other people. They candidly discern their own compromises and shortcomings first to see if their own wrong behaviors are contributing to their ideas on things.

3. *Know the signs of a seducing spirit.* Discerning believers understand that demons are subtle. When they show up, they may not look like a demon, so they know the traps that these demons use to deceive.

4. *Constantly sharpen your discernment.* We need regular sharpening by spending time in the Word of God, praying in the spirit, and being accountable. Before forming opinions, first make sure you have exercised the proper techniques for using discernment.

5. *Know how to test doctrine and interpret Scripture.* Many Christians point the finger, get deceived, or miss out on a blessing all because they don't know how to test doctrine correctly or interpret Scripture.

6. *Be aware of modern-day doctrines, fads, or trends.* Whenever a trend, teaching, movie, book, or similar fad is rising in quick popularity or is receiving new and expanded interest, it's worth filtering through. Popularity doesn't determine if it's good or bad, it just means we should take a second look. The Spirit of God can cause something to prosper exponentially, but so can demons. Use the other skills for discernment to look at it first before you jump on board.

With these skills in view, we can better examine the subject of recognizing a good pastor or ministry leader.

DIFFERENT CHURCHES, DIFFERENT FLAVORS

Realize that not every pastor, ministry, or leader may be your flavor. My husband once made a comment that I think is so true. He said, "Churches and pastors are like ice cream. There are countless flavors; some we like and some we don't, but they are all still ice cream." How true that is!

What we have to remember is that just because a pastor or church isn't our particular flavor doesn't make it a bad one.

Many years ago we had a man visit our church. He wasn't Spirit-filled, nor was he at all interested in such a thing. The only reason he came to church that day was because one of his relatives attended and had convinced this man to at least visit once. The day he came my husband was preaching on Psalm 91. He went down the chapter verse by verse and talked about how God protects us from the evil plans of the enemy. Truthfully, there was nothing controversial about it; he just preached each verse and expounded on what was written there.

The man visiting later told his relative that he didn't like the preaching at all. He said, "I didn't care for this man's message because it was too focused on the devil." He had many other points of criticism as well. He went further on to discredit the church and at one point even emailed us with all sorts of character insults and unfounded accusations. What was really driving him was the fact that he didn't want his relative attending the church because it was Spirit-filled and really just wasn't his flavor.

In our experience as pastors, we have had many people visit who didn't come back for similar miniscule reasons. We have also had some who've been in the church for quite some time and leave the church. In countless situations, we knew the motive behind their leaving was honestly because they didn't want to be held accountable for hidden sin or they refused to be obedient to the Bible in a certain area. Therefore, in order to make their leaving look justifiable they have to come up with a flaw in the pastor, church people, or church itself. More often their criticism is with the pastor or leadership. They will usually discredit something in his personality, something he or she said, or in some cases make the pastor out to be a real bad character.

Sometimes when this has happened, other people in the church who were their friends or family would look on and say, "Why would they leave? They were such good people; I wonder what the pastor did to hurt them?" More often than not in churches, people assume the pastor or church did something wrong rather than consider that the person who left may have had issues they may not be aware of. Many times as pastors, we have known information about the person who left which the congregation, close friends, and even family members didn't know. Often years later, the fruit of their lives reveals itself.

This is why as a church member you need to know the traits of a good pastor. Sure, no pastor is perfect, and no Christian is perfect. Human fault or simple limitations will play somehow into *every* situation, so we have to be careful we don't conclude opinions about things based on that. If a pastor has the correct character traits in place on a wide basis then you are likely looking at a good pastor, even when that pastor is not your particular flavor.

SEVEN CHARACTER TRAITS OF A GOOD PASTOR

If you can discern the character traits of a good pastor—not just in relation to you own pastor, but as you view all ministers and pastors—you will have a better view on church. You will be better prepared to filter through what you should and shouldn't listen to as things circulate the Body of Christ. Then when friends, family, and neighbors voice criticism, you can accurately stand up for the pastor or minister in question and steer them in the right direction.

I want to admonish readers here that good pastors need your support and encouragement. We will discuss wrong leaders and church accountability shortly, but for this section I want to defend your pastor's need for your support and gratitude. Pastors, itinerant ministers, and church leaders stand before audiences constantly. People examine everything from their clothes to their hair, their weight, and their age. They applaud their good sermons and critique their not so good sermons. People examine the pastor's family and the car he or she drives. They often see them on off days or when they are feeling under the weather. People form mental opinions about almost everything the pastor does—good and bad. That's just human nature; we like to form opinions about people!

Pastors are not just under the microscope from one or two people but the entire church, and sometimes, depending on the size of their ministry, the nation and the world. In addition to that, they are marked by the devil as a primary target.

Never underestimate the pastor's need for your help, prayers, and overall supportive attitude. Any pastor or leader becomes more successful when the people who participate in their ministry help undergird them in various ways. If your pastor (or any other ministry leaders you receive from) exhibits the constant fruit of the character traits we are about to review, get behind them and pray for them. They will become an even more effective leader.

These character traits of good leaders are woven all through the Bible which are:

1. He or she will take account of the state of the flock.

2. He or she will put themselves on the line in order to protect the sheep.

3. A good pastor feeds the sheep.

4. A good pastor provides a place of healing.

5. Good pastors take a stand for truth and righteousness.

6. Good pastors set the example.

7.   A good pastor embraces the anointing and presence of God.

THE STATE OF THE FLOCK

Good pastors are attentive to the needs of the sheep (see Prov. 27:23). They are always looking for ways within the church's ability to increase ministry effectiveness. However, a caring pastor also won't expend time, money, and volunteer hours just because it's what a small handful or one person asks for, nor do they add it because that's what other churches have. He will look at the big picture and make sure people are involved and doing their part, but not overly busy with unnecessary areas of ministry.

Good pastors also want the sheep to feel their gifts and talents are being useful. That doesn't mean there is always a place or opening for what everybody might feel the most "called" to do.

We have had people who came to our church with a heart for a certain area of ministry, sometimes one we didn't presently have. We usually will tell them to wait on the Lord, and if they are really called to it their gifts will eventually make room for them. Plus, new-comers especially should prove themselves in character, stability, and faith before they are handed the reins of a new arm of ministry. We encourage them to get involved in an area we already have and grow from there. Pastors need people who are willing to make successful the departments already in place. God has an amazing way of making sure your areas of gifting will reach their potential when you willingly do whatever is needed.

Pastors will also make sure the sheep are healthy and free of sin, infection, and disease. They will keep tabs when large rumors fly through the church, watching for problems that become widespread. If the pastor knows everyone has been sick one week, he is sensitive to the issue and may hold a healing service. If he or she sees that a large number of people are struggling with finances, he might teach on the subject. Good pastors care for the flock.

PROTECT THE SHEEP

A good pastor is willing to take unfair criticism, accept increased inconvenience and demand, do without, or even face confrontation rather than place excess burden on the sheep. He is also willing to put his own reputation on the line and risk being misunderstood in order to confront wolves (see Amos 3:12). Good pastors aren't afraid to deal with problems, even when the potential exists for onlookers (who often don't know all the facts) to misunderstand their motives.

He will be quick to put his own resources, time, and energy up in order to keep the sheep from excess burden. A good example I like to use here is that if the church holds a luncheon that charges people a cost, the pastor is willing to pay the same cost even if it's his job to be there. Now the church may not expect him to pay, but he always wants to do his part to alleviate the burden. If there is a special offering received, the pastor leads the way in giving as well. Good pastors aren't afraid to roll up their sleeves and work hard, both in ways that are obvious to people and in things behind the scenes that people may never see.

FEED THE SHEEP

A good pastor will make sure the sheep are receiving a well-rounded "meal" from the Bible (see 1 Peter 5:2). He will present the Scripture without shame, without partiality, and with depth. He or she will present the Word with both compassion and correction and won't be afraid to let the Bible speak for itself even when it may not be popular.

A good pastor will feed the sheep the Word in ministry outreach, programs, discipleship, printed material, and so on. He wants people to have a good working knowledge of the Scripture, a sound approach to doctrine, and to be spiritually mature.

He or she will present both milk and meat. Some people will go to a church and complain that it is either too shallow or too deep. Pastors make sure there is something for people at all different levels of growth and development.

For example, some churches spend all their time teaching on family and witnessing, while others are all about spiritual warfare and the prophetic. Now, just because a church leans heavily in one area or another doesn't mean the pastor isn't a good pastor, but he should provide the important things people need for spiritual growth at all levels. For example, some people don't need another lesson on how to prophesy, they need to learn to manage their finances and keep their children in order. Others don't need another lesson on how to be a loving Christian, they need to learn to pray deliverance and prophesy! A good pastor will make sure people are receiving a rich Word that addresses a wide variety of areas.

Additionally, a good pastor isn't afraid to feed the sheep the truth, even when the food he or she has to give may not be popular. If your pastor preaches against sin or on something that steps on your toes, don't be quick to jump into criticism just because your heart was convicted. Be teachable, and let your pastor feed you the honest and biblical truth and be thankful for it.

PROVIDE A PLACE OF HEALING

Good pastors show concern for the sick and broken and make this a priority in the church (see Luke 4:18; James 5:14-15). They provide prayer for the sick, ministry to the brokenhearted, and places for life skill development and personal care for general human needs.

They will raise up leaders and people in the church that can be their arms extended to help aid in this task.

Included in providing a place for healing is spiritual guidance and avenues for biblical counseling. There may also be means for people to receive deliverance and even resources for rehabilitation. This can include outreach through missions and feeding the hungry. Of course, while all churches are at different sizes and have different resources for creating these avenues, a good pastor will have the methods that work in his church for providing healing to the hurting.

STAND FOR TRUTH AND RIGHTEOUSNESS

This means he or she will take a strong biblical stance in the face of those who refuse holy living and sound doctrine. He will endure criticism in order to stand up for the Word of God and for what is right (see 2 Tim. 4:1-5).

Good pastors aren't afraid to confront sin and compromise and measure it against the Scripture, even at the risk of someone leaving the church. They will command their flocks to walk in righteousness, not make it sound like a suggestion or optional decision.

This also means that, at times, pastors will have to confront wolves. Sometimes we get the wrong idea that everyone is welcome in our churches. Well, yes, we welcome everyone who wants to come and allows themselves to be moldable in the hands of the Holy Spirit and walk in Christian unity. However, good pastors shouldn't allow wolves to run rampant, stirring up strife or luring people into sin. A good pastor will send the wolves who want to hurt the sheep packing!

If a man comes into the church who wants to prey upon the young women by looking at them inappropriately or by luring them into compromise, then a good pastor will correct him. When some want to gain a ministry position and draw people to themselves until it diminishes people's respect for their pastor, then it should be addressed. If someone comes to the church and takes advantage of well-meaning people through dishonest business practices, then the pastor has the authority to speak up.

Be careful you aren't too quick to assume your pastor is being too harsh when he has to correct an issue. A large number of Christians are too quick to assume because either they think it's inappropriate for a pastor to exercise correction or they form opinions without all the facts. Some erroneously think pastors should be *so* loving to the point that they allow just about any behavior in the church. They can't wrongly assume that pastors who correct things are somehow acting out of line or are not accountable. Good pastors will correct, command righteousness, and deal with issues. This is an important ingredient to loving the flock and is a biblical expectation for a true shepherd.

SET THE EXAMPLE

He or she doesn't expect their people to do what they aren't willing to do, such as work hard for the Kingdom, follow truth, tithe, and walk in the spirit of love and purity. He exhibits through word and actions to people that he is willing to grow in his Christianity as much as they are. He or she will strive to live what they preach (see 1 Tim. 4:12).

The reason many pastors lose respect is they expect their people to come to church on time while they come 30 minutes late. They want the people to work hard to build the vision, but they don't give as much time as the people do.

Good pastors lead by example. If they expect their sheep to have Christian accountability, they make sure they have accountability with other pastors and overseers. If they want the people to read their Bible, then they make a habit of Bible reading, and so on. A good pastor puts the needs of the church before his own.

EMBRACES THE ANOINTING AND PRESENCE OF GOD

A good pastor will love the presence of God more than a religious environment (see 2 Tim. 1:5). He or she will embrace the tangible power of the Holy Spirit so that lives can be touched, delivered, and set free. He will make room for the Holy Spirit to interrupt his agenda and allow the gifts of the Holy Spirit to be in manifestation at any time they are needed.

He will create the right environment that allows people to be expressive in worship or that encourages everyone to participate in a way that isn't flakey or confined to just one or two people. Instead, he or she encourages the whole body to step into the presence of God. A good pastor desires for the people to receive ministry from the Spirit that is supernatural and that is not limited to his or her natural pastoral ability.

THREE KINDS OF PASTORS OR MINISTERS TO AVOID

While I want in this chapter to focus on the character traits of *good* pastors, I also feel it is important to touch on some examples of the kind of pastors or other ministers you may want to avoid. After all, that is what discernment really is—it's separating the good from the bad.

There is a lot of chatter these days about pastors who have given the ministry a bad name. You constantly hear the words "abuse" and "control" in reference to ministries. Of course, there are leaders who have fallen from ministry and have led innocent people astray or abused their position of leadership. We will talk about the warning signs of these types of ministers.

First, however, I briefly want to clarify what truly makes a pastor or other minister the kind to avoid. While exploring every problem issue along these lines would be too extensive here, a few simple points will help you discern when a leader might be off. Realize when I list these traits that they are the *overall* traits being exhibited that constantly seem to outweigh any good qualities. Just because a pastor or minister can reflect a few negatives every now and then as they are growing in their ministry, it doesn't automatically classify them as a pastor to avoid. Some of their occasional negatives may even mimic what classifies the wrong type of pastor. However, a pastor who has solid ministry fruit, is respected among other pastors and church leaders, and has a solid congregation that fits into sound Christianity probably isn't a bad or dangerous leader. A leader becomes one to avoid when the negatives start to come to the constant forefront and begin to overshadow the good things on a *continual* basis.

When this happens, these pastors or ministers will usually start to carry an overall persona that just feels wrong. You will start to notice the negative traits are more pronounced, and it begins to be what represents them in most of what they do.

I say all this because many believers have left churches pointing the finger of accusation and making the pastor look like some kind of charlatan. But with further investigation, in many situations that wasn't the case at all. Often it was because the pastor confronted them on an issue of lying or adultery, so to cover it up they made the pastor out to have evil character and said he was mistreating them. In some cases, the pastor just held them accountable for a bad attitude or lack of commitment or simply asked them to work in the nursery. That's when they left shouting "abuse," creating all sorts of convincing stories.

Examples of wrong pastors can be seen throughout Ezekiel 34. While we don't want to write out the entire chapter here, we will pull these examples from the chapter. First look at verse 2. It says:

> *Son of man, prophesy against the shepherds of Israel,*
> *prophesy, and say unto them, Thus saith the Lord*

God unto the shepherds; Woe be to the shepherds of Israel that do feed themselves! Should not the shepherds feed the flocks? (Ezekiel 34:2)

Even when the wrong or abusive pastors exhibit no accountability, never underestimate God's ability to keep them in check! If God says the word "woe" to someone, it's a bad thing! These kinds of pastors will eventually suffer the consequences for mishandling their ministries, even if they deliberately avoided any natural system of accountability. From the rest of Ezekiel 34, we find several characteristics of the pastors or ministers that we need to avoid.

THE SELF-COMFORTED PASTOR

They feed themselves, but don't feed the sheep (see Ezek. 34:3). For example, there are pastors who have all sorts of excessive personal needs or co-dependent behaviors. They have high expectations and determined efforts for meeting their own personal, spiritual, or emotional needs, wants, or desires, and they will expect people to provide it for them as their "duty." They always make sure they personally are well-fed, ministered to, and cared for, but they spend little time making sure the people are doing OK. At the same time, they give the sheep a watered down message, put in little time and effort, and present a shoddily run ministry with little visible development of any life-changing ministry programs that truly feed the people.

Many of these pastors have standards for the people which they don't hold themselves accountable to. They carry themselves as if the ministry makes them exempt from having certain basic ethics or principles. For example, some pastors are rude and unmannerly in the way they treat their workers, but they want everybody to be respectful of them. I have heard pastors order people around very correctively right from the platform while ministering. Their attitudes, voice tones, and behavior are in poor taste. When Jesus corrected people, sometimes even publically in His ministry, it was because there was deliberate continual unbelief, rebellion, or religious defiance. It wasn't when good-hearted people were working tirelessly to serve the vision but were not doing every little thing just the way He demanded.

I very much understand when a service is going on from the platform that it takes sharp people to make the ministry be the most effective. You need sharp ushers that can organize people receiving prayer or musicians and sound people that can keep the service running smoothly. However, I also think of the missionary preacher who has none of these bells and whistles and can step into the anointing of God without any air conditioning or platform perfection, yet these are seeing creative miracles of healing just the same.

Pastors cannot make their own comfort the predominant focus. While they legitimately need people to help them and serve their ministry vision, they also cannot place their personal needs at such a high priority that they step on others.

THE ABUSIVE/CONTROLLING PASTOR

These ignore helping the sick, poor, needy, and lost, but instead make excessive demands from them (see Ezek. 34:4). These are pastors who develop almost no ministry for the needy in the church, but in turn enforce ridiculous demands from the very needy that they ignore, such as imposing rights to their personal property or family or expecting or manipulating excessive or lucrative personal gifts such as a car, pricey jewelry, or house. These pastors overlook the people's family needs and expect them to give, work, and produce sacrificially far beyond what is taught in Scripture, and usually that sacrifice has less to do with advancing the church and more to do with catering to the excessive personal lifestyle needs of the pastor.

These pastors will usually exhibit little effort to reach the lost or encourage soul winning. They are only concerned with garnering a group of people that help build their platform. Some of these pastors even abuse the ministry by going so far as to deliberately justify certain sinful lifestyles.

From a different angle, some pastors are so demanding that their people or staff can't be away from the phone even in the middle of the night. Now I understand that the nature of the ministry might require the occasional after-hours call or for someone to go above and beyond the call of duty. Those occasions cannot always be helped. However, people need a break from everything church and should feel like they can take a long bath without having to feel the church leadership or pastor is going to call and ask them to do something. This seems to be a larger problem in the Charismatic churches because there is such an emphasis on having a heart for the Kingdom and making sacrifices. Yes, sacrifice is required of all of us, but at the same time people need to rest and have time for a normal family home life so they can remain effective Christians. Pastors cannot be extremely demanding beccause this can get over into abusive behavior.

It is important that Christians know the *true* signs of control. Control is not because the pastor held you accountable or confronted a sin issue. Control is when the requirements from the pastor diminish any ability to have a normal life outside constant pastoral demand. This kind of demand is different from the pastor's expectation for people to have biblical boundaries, sound commitment to church involvement, or just to reach out to people on a daily basis. Instead, it involves *extreme* things like not being able to make independent decisions on your budget or what car you drive. True control usually can be seen in that it *over*-interferes with the home structure by preventing families from having any sense of independence to work out their personal salvation. A good pastor cannot police the sheep and have his hands in every minute detail of people's lives.

THE COWARDLY PASTOR

They allow the sheep to be scattered and become prey to wolves and deceivers (see Ezek. 34:5-6). These are pastors who make no effort to stand up against wrongdoing in the church or protect the sheep from deception. This pastor is political and afraid to stand against division, wolves, sin, and unruly behavior for fear of making enemies or just to save his own reputation. This pastor doesn't want to deal with the misbehavior or sin of "brother big-bucks" because he might leave the church! He fears losing members so he essentially lets people do whatever they feel, often at the expense of others getting hurt. He has no backbone, and people in that church often become disorderly and eventually fall prey to various temptations, demonic bondages, and lying spirits that can ultimately affect their very salvation.

SEVEN CHARACTER TRAITS OF TRUE AND MATURE SHEEP

Even though this chapter is about discerning the signs of a good pastor and church, the reason many struggle with this is because they lack certain character traits also needed for being mature sheep. Immaturity can keep you from discerning if your pastor is a quality pastor and can reduce your ability to have a good experience in any church.

Paul told Timothy that he and the people he leads should know that there is a right and wrong way to conduct themselves as members in God's household, and part of that includes conduct in churches.

But if I tarry long, that thou mayest know how thou ought to behave thyself in the house of God, which is the church of the living God, the pillar and ground of the truth (1 Timothy 3:15).

The following will help you discern if you have the signs of a good sheep or church member.

1. *When sheep know they have a good pastor, they are supportive of him/her* (see John 10:3). A true sheep will listen to the pastor because they will trust that his or her only motive is to help them become all they can be for the Kingdom of God and grow as a Christian. They will have a good attitude in the church and get involved in the things the pastor makes available in the church. They will also receive biblical correction if and when it is needed.

2. *Mature sheep work to grow in their Christianity* (see Phil. 2:12). This means they will take godly character and righteousness seriously. They make Bible reading, prayer, and church commitment a priority in their life. They take Christianity seriously in choosing their family activities, entertainment, appearance, and associations. They avoid sin.

3. *They are not divisive and rebellious. They stay unified with other sheep and with the leadership* (see 1 Cor. 3:3). True sheep avoid things that create division in the church. They would rather take a back seat of applause than discredit someone else. They encourage others to shine over them. They don't capitalize on little reasons to complain or voice disagreement. Instead, they would rather look for reasons to support projects, departments, and events in

the church rather than create reason to dispute them. They don't gossip or listen to rumors about the leadership or fellow believers.

4. *They are content and consistent, not high-maintenance* (see 1 Tim. 6:6). True sheep are not overly needy. They don't always need someone in the church or another pastoral appointment to keep them in the game. They aren't always in need of a phone call by a deacon in order to feel special. Of course, these things are fine on occasion, but a true sheep is normally content with the "pasture" the pastor is feeding them through all the church's many venues of ministry. They are stable Christians who walk in the spirit, not after the flesh.

5. *True sheep accept and use the established channels of authority* (see John 10:1-2). True sheep aren't always finding ways to "go around the system." They accept the established procedures and policies and see them as an aid to create order and flow. They don't undermine the pastors, staff, or department heads to get what they want, prove a point, or create their own platform.

6. *They trust their shepherd/pastor over the voices of "strangers"* (see 2 Tim. 3:14). They believe in their pastor's fruit and character and are not quick to draw attention to his faults or believe criticism, gossip, and negative comments people may say of him. In their mind, their

pastor's godly character speaks for itself and outweighs his faults. They also are confident of their pastor's judgment when it comes to people because of his sound track record that is reflected in the overall health of the church itself.

7. *They willingly offer their resources, time, and effort for the Kingdom and the ministry* (see Luke 8:3). These sheep tithe, give offerings, and put their time and effort into the eternal purpose of the ministry. They see the work of the church as vital for changing lives and winning the lost. They are more willing to give than to complain about giving. They are happy to be involved and consider it a privilege.

CHURCH ACCOUNTABILITY

Everyone needs some accountability. Many Christians who attend church want the pastor to be held accountable for everything he does, but they don't want him to hold them accountable for anything. On the other hand, some pastors demand the people be accountable, while they never exhibit the same effort in their own lives.

I do want to clarify and bring a balance to the issue of human accountability. In some circles it is overemphasized, while in others there is none at all or there is a lose version of it at best. There are both pastors and church people who create extreme expectations for accountability. Human accountability, no matter how "perfect" the system might be, cannot and will never replace accountability to God.

I understand there is a big deception in some people who go around claiming, "I am accountable to no man, only to God!" They don't understand that if you study the life of the great apostle Paul, you will find he made his ministry accountable to other apostles and submitted revelation for their review (see Acts 15:2; 13-22; Gal. 1:17-19; 2:1-2). So I believe deeply in the need for human accountability for both pastors and church people. Briefly, here are a few ways both pastors and church members can create human accountability.

PASTORS	CHURCH MEMBERS
A Pastor/Spiritual Father—Even in the ministry, a pastor still needs a pastor to talk to and help speak into his life. A pastor will talk to a pastor about his character, ministry ethics, and practices.	A Pastor/Elders—This can be the senior pastor, associate pastors, and also appointed church leaders. It should be direct and indirect through various forms of conversation, involvement, and church attendance.
Ministerial Colleagues and Friends—Pastors should develop relationships with others in the ministry, whether locally or nationally, who he can call and get advice from and share concerns with.	Department Heads or Deacons—By staying closely involved in the church under certain department heads, a believer can create accountability allowing attitude, attendance, and lifestyle to be more easily seen.
A Ministerial Board—Pastors should have a ministerial board, preferably consisting of other experienced ministers, which is in line with Scripture.	Committed Involvement and Attendance—Regular attendance of church services and various activities helps believers show commitment to the Kingdom.

PASTORS	CHURCH MEMBERS
Ministerial Staff—Associate pastors or similar staff can help create accountability by helping the pastor develop safe and secure business operations and management.	Christians—Making a habit of being around solid and stable Christians creates accountability and helps propel believers to make a habit of living strong for God.

At the same time, I also realize that human accountability won't solve every issue, and we can't use it to replace God's ability to hold people accountable. Truly, whatever we sow, we will eventually reap. There are consequences to wrongdoing that will come into full manifestation and without repentance will eventually get exposed. I have seen pastors lose ministries and even their lives for mishandling the ministry. I have seen quality Christians lose the same. God held people accountable in the Bible and is well able to keep His Church accountable today. I don't want the need for human accountability to make any of us think that God isn't capable of holding people accountable, nor should any of us, whether pastor or Christian, over-emphasize human accountability. If we do, we can all run the risk of trying to be the Holy Spirit. Pastors can't exhaust themselves trying to police every detail of their church members' lives, while the congregation can't live speculating if the pastor is making his every move accountable to some man-made system.

WHY WE ALL NEED A CHURCH

No church is perfect. If there are two human beings in a room there will be fault. No pastor is perfect, and no church member is perfect. We can't set ourselves up for disappointment because we have unreasonable expectations for what we think a church should or shouldn't be like. However, perfect or not, never underestimate the important need for attending and getting involved in a church.

There is a large movement today that minimizes the need for the traditional church model. Before we touch on that, I know from experience that everyone's situation and ability to connect to a church is different. Years ago, I always preached that *everyone* needs to be at church every time the doors are open! Then I realized that really what God is looking for is involvement coupled with consistency that shows self-sacrifice. This varies slightly from family to family.

For example, we have a couple in our church who has attended since we started. They are farmers who live over an hour and a half away. They come almost every Sunday and attend special events. However, beyond that there isn't much more they can do because they live too far away. Living on a farm requires them to drive quite a distance to find a church.

There are always some unique situations like this that prevent some people from being able to give the kind of commitment that it takes to build the high-impact church. Nevertheless, these are usually the exceptions.

I don't want anyone to discount the truth of needing to get deeply involved in church because there are valid exceptions otherwise. Most people should work hard to find a good church and put their roots down there, even if there are legitimate variations in their involvement.

The Bible speaks repeatedly about the importance of the corporate church. Dangerously, some Christians have fallen into error because they didn't discern their need for a good church or pastor. Some today believe you don't need the traditional model of a church to have "church." They feel it's just as acceptable to have church with a few friends in your living room. While that *can* be a valid gathering, I don't think it can eliminate the need for the congregational church model. Acts says:

And they, continuing daily with one accord in the temple, and breaking bread from house to house, did eat their meat with gladness and singleness of heart (Acts 2:46).

We see here that the early church had both. They had the corporate experience of meeting together in the temple or public location as well as meeting together house to house (see Luke 24:53).

As we remain discerning in the last days, we need to remind ourselves that churches are a lifeline of safety for the believer. We learn from the Scriptures that there were special anointings that were strictly upon the corporate gatherings or public types of meetings (see 2 Chron. 5:13-14; Acts 4:23-32). Think about it—there was the cloud of glory that descended upon the tabernacle of meeting. There was the anointing on Jesus' ministry and also the apostle Paul that healed multitudes of people (see Matt. 5:1-2; Acts 19:10-12).

There is something about the corporate gathering in public locations that creates an atmosphere. It's different than the few gathered around a table. It's strong and more powerful. We call it the corporate anointing, and I wouldn't trade it for anything!

The corporate anointing has a unique power for breaking yokes of bondage off people's lives. In a good church, there is an aura of God that fills the room when all the people come together, lifting their hands to the Lord as the musicians begin to play. There is a sense of safety and stability when the pastor stands up before the people to declare the Word of God. You can't exchange the sensation that comes as you see people you hardly know get touched through the ministry of the Holy Spirit.

Every believer needs this type of anointing on an ongoing basis. Christians who allow themselves to be regularly exposed to the corporate atmosphere tend to have a more balanced view on things. That is because they are used to dealing with people of all varying types. That experience causes people to step outside themselves, come out of their shell, and learn to adapt to the differences in others.

People who only gather around a video at home or with the same handful of friends each week are missing out on the more powerful, corporate experience. Sure home groups have their dimension, but they need to come under the umbrella of the larger corporate anointing that helps make well-rounded believers who can adapt to various settings. The setting forces you to adjust when you sit by people you don't know or perhaps didn't interact with last Sunday. You learn how to be more agreeable when you plant yourself in a church because you quickly realize that not everyone is like you!

I love the corporate anointing. There have been countless times I have worked all day in ministry and was exhausted by the end of the day. But I went to church that same night, and the moment we entered the presence of God I was strengthened. There is just something about it. Initially, I wanted to go home and rest, but afterwards I was a new person! That is what church does for you.

Church also provides you friends and help during your times of challenge. You can always be confident that in a good church there are people to walk you through your trials. Many Christians who have left off going to church find themselves all alone when they are under attack. Not in every situation is there anyone from their small handful of friends available. From there they have no one else to call. In the last days, this is not where were we want to find ourselves, because the Bible teaches us to discern that these are dangerous times.

It's also hard to backslide when on-fire believers are standing next to you worshiping God with all their hearts. A good church will keep you straight and on track as a Christian if you will put your roots down and get connected. Sure, you might not agree with everything or everyone, but face it—they won't all agree with you either! No church is perfect, but we need one anyhow. The churches of the Bible weren't perfect either, thus the reason Paul had to admonish them! Nonetheless, the church environment helps you grow and flourish as a Christian. Psalms says, *"Those that be planted in the house of the Lord shall flourish in the courts of our God"* (Ps. 92:13).

Some people aren't flourishing today because they didn't discern how important the local church was to their stability. The body of believers in your church under the loving guidance of the pastor and leaders acts as a safety net during the last days. No matter what you have been through or what your negative church experiences have been, get into a church. As the last days heat up, you will find safety in the numbers it provides. The church is a bulwark of defense against the powers of darkness, and there is simply no way to believe otherwise. Don't let hurt feelings or rebellion and reasoning keep you from putting your roots down in a church home.

As we grow in spiritual discernment, let's make sure we know the traits of good pastors and ministers. Let's discern the importance of the local church. This awareness will enable us to recognize the schemes of the devil that would want to drive us out of good churches. That is not where we want to be found. Remember:

> *Not forsaking the assembling of ourselves together, as the manner of some is; but exhorting one another: and so much the more, as ye see the day approaching* (Hebrews 10:25).

Let's discern the necessity of a good pastor and good church in the last days!

Chapter Nine

DISCERNING THE DANGERS AND TEMPTATIONS ON THE MEDIA HIGHWAY

There hath no temptation taken you but such
as is common to man: but God is faithful,
who will not suffer you to be tempted above
that ye are able; but will with the temptation
also make a way to escape, that ye may
be able to bear it (1 Corinthians 10:13).

"**M**om, I want a cell phone!" "Can I create a Facebook?" "Hey Dad, all my friends have the action figures from that movie, can I have 'em?" "Mom, I need that new jacket 'cause the stars on television wear it!" "Hey! We need more cable channels!" "I just have to have that video game; it only takes the Lord's name in vain a few times!" "Come on Dad, all my friends are going to that show!"

These are all the things these days we hear coming from kids and teens. But the pull driven by a media-immersed society doesn't stop with them. It exists on a different level for the adults.

"Hey, it's a good movie; there's only one sex scene." "I like to watch that show so I can stay informed!" "I don't have time to go to the theater; that's why I get all the move channels." "Oh, sci-fi is fine; you just have to realize it isn't real." "It doesn't cost that much; I really need that new big screen." "The book really isn't all that bad if you can look past a few things." "Man, if I just win the lottery, I'd give the money to the church!"

Do these comments sound familiar to you?

The most powerfully discerning Christian needs to learn the skills for defeating the modern temptations easily fed into our minds through the media and online world. They are coming right through our cell phones, laptops, television screens, and gaming systems. Many of these temptations are coming with unrelenting force through these digital means.

The worldly atmosphere and worldly point of view is so readily available in the four walls of our own homes, and many Christians are losing discernment regarding it. The digital world dramatically increases the potential for these dangers simply because they are so convenient. We can become so easily softened to new ideals imparted through the power of media. Because the color and sound of modern media's influence is so emotionally moving and captivating, it can be one of the easiest methods for falling prey to deception.

Not only are these media venues available in our homes, but the pressure you feel these days is to have all the latest toys. Technology is updated almost monthly. Just about the time you buy a new cell phone, the next one comes out and your co-worker is showing you all the things theirs can do that yours can't! Electronics can do almost anything we want. Today you don't just watch television; you record all your favorite shows on DVR. You can watch one show while another records, and you can view two channels at once. No longer do you have 50 channels to view; there are several hundred. Movies can even be rented from the convenience and privacy of your own home.

Cell phones are no longer just for making calls. They are used to access the Internet, text and chat, send data, read attachments, and take photos. You can almost house a complete office in the palm of your hand. This onslaught by the media world begs us to perk up our senses of discernment. It seems Christians are almost at the mercy of a media tidal wave. As a result, there is increased debate about what material should be considered acceptable for believers. The argument about what secular entertainment a Christian should and shouldn't enjoy isn't new. What is more recent is the enormous mass of avenues that media has available to flood its way into our lives every single day, all day long. Somewhere, it's a warning sign that our discerning spirit on this issue alone has to be even more alert.

A sign that your discernment has become dull is when you begin to justify too many of these modern media things and have to create reasons why they are acceptable activities. Many Christian groups and schools are using certain sci-fi and fantasy programming as resources for teaching Christian values. In some cases, they are going overboard to prove how these films and storybooks have a "Christian" comparison or analogy when they are often filled with some of the most obvious forms of black magic.

Now, is this to say we need to throw our televisions and laptops in the dumpster? I don't think so. What it means again is we need to exercise sharp discernment so we can separate the evil from the good without compromising the kind of standards that God lays out in Scripture in a day when it would be so easy to become confused.

POWER IN LIMITATIONS

As a parent, I have found that it is nearly impossible today for my children to enjoy any form of entertainment, games, or movies without crossing paths with some form of worldly influence or even downright inappropriate information. I mean, you can hardly get a paper cup at the drive thru without it having an image of the latest movie character, some of them downright demonic. Toys are plastered with occult symbols and nearly all video games have something less desirable by Christian parents who want to train their children in righteousness. Even the most basic of sports games are filled with secular images and questionable rap music. Even though some of these things come with ratings and parental control or on and off options, it's still unavoidable. The things meant for the youngest of kids are inundated with anti-Christian themes.

We are almost at a point where we can either have almost no media entertainment or we have to discern a way to keep our entertainment indulgences in check. This begins with limiting all forms of these media sources. Of course, when we think of this, we usually first consider the kids and their video games and just limiting overall television watching. However, what seems impossible is limiting time on our cell phones and laptops. Really? Can we go a day without any of these things? Are you serious?

However, we have to once again use discernment. Of course, many of these things are tools necessary to functioning in the modern world. Modern society has become dependent on these digital technologies and mobile devices. I mean, I couldn't imagine writing this very book with a pencil or a typewriter! I probably couldn't even have done it on a desktop computer. Thank God for the mobility of the laptop! However, the same laptops that help us accomplish a lot of work also help us spend plenty of time shopping the online stores and reading the news or other Internet stories. This means we need to have some boundaries.

I am thrilled to have a cell phone because I can stay aware of my family's whereabouts. But cell phone contact has its drawbacks. Usually, I try to remember to turn my cell phone off when we are asleep at night, but there have been times I have forgotten and received a call or text alert in the middle of the night. Wouldn't you know it, my sleep is totally disrupted and affected for the next two hours. Some pastors and friends I know never turn their cell phones off. They are on them 24/7. That means even when not taking calls one is mentally invaded by the constant interruption.

Let's take the time to discern the many effects that constant time connected to media devices is having on our lives.

1. Stolen time from God

Realistically, there are many times we could have prayed longer in the morning, but it was that extra time reading the news online that forced us to shorten it. Sometimes there are good intentions for some Bible study time, but there was another marathon of your favorite television show or you just had to clean out your inbox. We don't need to expound too long on this point. We all know the times when God has taken a back seat to our media interests.

2. Inability for time alone

It seems you can hardly take a shower without someone expecting you to answer your cell. Cell phones, as wonderful as they are, have made everyone who knows you believe you are always in the presence of your phone. People expect you to answer it no matter where you are or what you're doing. Then beyond the calls are the texts and emails via the phone. Sure, you clear the last messages off, and moments later the thing is beeping again or flashing to say you have another email.

We need time alone to collect our thoughts. Every person needs a few waking hours away from the influence of the outside, and media devices are often preventing an opportunity for us to have it.

3. Increased Stress

Always staying connected to the cell phone world, Internet world, and television world is increasing our stress levels. We always feel like we have something to process mentally, someone we have to get back to, or the pressure to work on some project. Even the news home pages that give us good pointers about taking care of our health or bettering our finances are filling our minds with one more thing we know we need to do.

4. Less time with family

Families spend less time together with so many media outlets. Gone are the days of the family television—now we have televisions, gaming systems, and computers in several rooms of the house! Each person easily makes their way to the media venue of choice, and in moments we're connected. Often, this occurs in separate rooms with little interaction with the others in the house. This is causing families to communicate less and do things together less often.

5. Excess work overload

With media technology, many employees don't even physically have to go to their office. They can remote in right from home and do their work, and for some it's a pretty close second to actually being there. The growing problem now is that some never quit working. They are up at all hours trying to get things done!

I have to tell on myself on this one. One night I was up working on my laptop well after midnight. Thinking no one would be up at that hour, I decided to send a few emails so people would have them first thing in the morning. To my surprise, one businessper-son responded to me immediately! They were even in a time zone that was later than mine, and I knew they weren't traveling in a different time zone. Like many these days, they were awake working at all hours.

Technology *has* afforded us the convenience of work at home, but now we never quit working.

6. Easier exposure to sin and vices

Years ago, it used to be if a person was going to watch a question-able movie or read questionable material, they had to go to a public place to obtain it. Those days are long gone. We don't have to spend time even discussing all the ways a person can use media devices for evil. With these things, the temptations for sin and compromise through the use of media are extremely magnified, and in many places it is destroying families, homes, and happiness.

7. Increased wasted time

Sometimes, we just use our media toys to waste time. It's that extra mindless game of Solitaire or the aimless Internet surfing when you know you really need to mow the lawn or finish the laundry. Then before you know it, your evening has expired and it's time to head off to bed. There is another time-wasting habit this creates as well, which is constant random glancing at your phone just to see if there was something new you missed. Many times, we know there might not have been anything, but constant habit causes us to grab the phone, take a peek, and push buttons.

8. Addiction to media pastimes

Even the most innocent of media pastimes can consume us. People are addicted. They are addicted to media inventions. When you ride in an airplane, people can hardly wait until the wheels touch the runway to turn their cell phones back on! As much as I travel, I shamefully admit that I am included in this group! You can hear all the little beeps and ringtones throughout the cabin as people get themselves back online. When you sit in the airport, you watch people totally tied to their devices. We have to watch addictions to media inventions.

9. High potential for demonic strongholds

Because there is so much information passed through media outlets, we also have to be careful about what kinds of ideals and influences are being imparted. There can be countless demonic images and influences attached to these devices, and we have to be careful that we don't let them build a stronghold in our lives.

10. Lowers interest in other important activities

Sometimes excessive use of electronic toys lowers people's interest in other healthful activities and can even hinder development of other key life skills. This is especially true with kids. They can literally spend hours playing a video game or watching television. Once becoming so deeply engrossed, it's hard to break away and work on other important things. Suddenly, they are not as interested in learning to help Mom cook in the kitchen or help work on a project with Dad. In some reports, excessive gaming has even been said to contribute to certain health problems. Many times, excessive use of these electronic forms of entertainment even keep people from doing other things they would normally enjoy.

11. Laziness and inactivity

A great deal has already been said about the inactivity these things create. Many people spend more time sitting down playing computer games or movie watching than engaging in some activity that promotes physical exercise.

12. *Lowered standards*

Often, the more you watch or hear something, the more "used" to it you become. This is most true in the media world. The more we hear cursing on television or the more we watch violent news reports or off-color entertainment, the more desensitized we become. Eventually, we lower our standards, and what once bothered us is no longer offensive.

13. *Too much of a worldly point of view*

The truth is that what we spend time listening to the most will eventually have the most influence in our lives. Many Christians spend more time hearing the world's perspective through the news, Internet, television, web pages, and more. Often we come in contact with these mediums more than we do our own Bibles. We have to watch the worldly influences that the media is known for. If we aren't careful, these things can deceptively warp our Christian ideals and change some of our godly views.

14. *Increased financial demands*

Here you have the cell phone bill, the Internet service costs, the price of the laptop, or the newest speaker system. Then, because electronics outdate so quickly, we always want the newer one every few months. Cell phone companies keep you coming back for new gadgets by offering upgrades and promotions. We have to consider the increased financial demands that come with all these items.

SAFETY ON THE MULTIMEDIA HIGHWAY

We can't fully consider the subject of spiritual discernment without considering the increasing ramifications the media generation is having on the church. Of course, it all comes back to being a Christian *in* the world but not being *of* the world. That wasn't easy to do thirty years ago, but make no mistake it is much harder now with our minds being exposed to so much more through the power of media technology. With the world so easily at our fingertips, we increase the possibility for embarking on a new kind of Christianity.

I believe there is no doubt as to the influence media is having on the Church corporately. The Christian influence on the media highway is a very miniscule percentage compared to the worldly control over it. Compared to thousands of worldly channels, you find a handful of Christian programs. Most world news isn't from a Christian perspective; it's from a worldly one. Most kids would rather play the latest sports games seen on television then some unknown game developed for Christians. The list goes on and on.

We are fooling ourselves to think the world's massive influence in technology and entertainment is not going to affect how Christians live or view the world. We simply spend too much time involved with it for it not to happen. As we discussed earlier, continual exposure leads to gradual acceptance.

At the same time, media technology holds many opportunities for preaching the Gospel, so it isn't the technology itself that presents the problem. The problem for the Church is a lack of discernment on how to use it without gradually lowering our standards. As technology increases and the world's standard upon it keeps getting lower, we need to make discerning decisions, lest we open ourselves up to the wrong influences. Colossians says:

> *Beware lest any man spoil you through philosophy and vain deceit, after the tradition of men, after the rudiments of the world, and not after Christ* (Colossians 2:8).

The *"rudiments of the world"* are simply the world's way of thinking, principles for life, and influence. The devil has a convenient opportunity to change our thinking to line up with the world through the means of technology. Therefore, the discerning believer in this media generation must discern how to use technology for good and even for fun at times, but still be able to stay alert and avoid the deceptive influence it has. By making some definite decisions, you can be safer on the multimedia highway and still keep your discernment skills intact. The problem is many Christians are not heightening their awareness but rather are lowering standards. With the large influx, we need to start drawing some serious lines in the sand. If not, we will slowly be lulled to sleep. It's like the old story of the frog in a boiling pot of water. If you threw the frog in some hot water, he would jump out. But if you put him in some cool water and slowly bring it to a boil, he will sit there unaware and boil to death.

> *But if ye will not drive out the inhabitants of the land from before you; then it shall come to pass, that those which ye let remain of them shall be pricks in your eyes, and thorns in your sides, and shall vex you in the land wherein ye dwell* (Numbers 33:55).

The need for discernment, now that we are immersed in the media generation, will become more paramount with each passing day. Be discerning by incorporating the following:

1. Set high standards and don't justify choices.

2. Have control or accountability methods in place.

3. Limit access and use.

4. Make your own personal decisions.

5. Have regular spiritual housecleaning.

SET HIGH STANDARDS

As we make choices on things such as entertainment, television watching, or Internet use, we need to set clear biblical standards. These standards can't be barely a step above the world. We need our standards to come up to the level of Scripture. One of the hardest things to do is say "no" to a movie or game that you would otherwise enjoy except for that one scene or few scenes or some of the movie lines.

We have to decide not to justify our choices. What I mean is that we can't come up with "good reasons" that make compromised standards appear justifiable. As I cited earlier, many Christians are actually taking secular movies with some promiscuous and even occult material and are making "Christian" messages out of them. In other words, they are looking for a spiritual lesson to be learned through these movies. While I am not saying a secular movie cannot ever contain a spiritual message to be learned, we cannot make a habit of this practice. I believe the reason some people do this is to justify why they include it in their entertainment choices.

We shouldn't justify our choices and make them more important than the standards of Scripture. When it comes to media entertainment or television, especially these days, lean on the side of extra prudence and discernment.

ACCOUNTABILITY METHODS

Taking advantage of things such as parental controls, channel blocking, Internet monitoring, or similar safeguards is a good idea just to promote safety, especially for children. However, we need to take our spiritual safeguards to another level.

In our home, we have a family standard during television watching. One person is on remote control duty. It is that person's job to watch for the bad commercials. These days it isn't always the actual program that's the problem. It's the movie trailers, commercials, and other ads. Certain medical ads promote more than just awareness; they also open the door to fear. There are countless ads with worldly themes, scantily dressed men and women, sinful activities, and more. In fact, it is no secret that a large majority of television commercials today are selling products by using sexual themes to promote them. We cannot allow these things to come into our "eye" and "ear" gates, or our Christian standards and values will become compromised. Develop family accountability and standards for using the television.

The same standards should be applied to the Internet. Many Christians don't pause to consider the impact of something before they get involved in an activity. Of course, with the obvious safeguards such as having site blocking programs or placing the family computer in full view, there are other important safeguards we as believers should add. For children, we need to not only add the parental control types of safeguards, but we need to give our kids instruction in righteousness when it comes to the Internet. Parents anymore have a harder time preventing their kids from always having contact with the online world in some form. We need to set accountability in these areas.

Then we as adults need to create our own safeguards online that show we are trustworthy. Husbands and wives can express an attitude of spousal accountability with Internet use. The idea is to show trustworthy behavior.

Some ideas might be leaving your laptop out and easily accessible while you are not home, knowing that if your spouse was to use it they would find a lengthy Internet history that is honorable. Of course, any method of accountability could be deviated from if one really wants to be deceptive, but the idea is to show that you are not secretive in any way and that you are setting obvious boundaries for yourself. For example, if something inappropriate did happen to pop up during a search, then tell your spouse immediately. Things like this show others that you are committed to putting your own methods of control in place.

Certain computer habits can give the impression that you are secretive, such as habitual late night computer use while your spouse is sleeping. Another practice that might make you appear secretive might be a lack of openness with emails or text messages. While I am not saying you need to report every message, certain behaviors like never wanting your spouse to borrow your phone could give the wrong appearance even if innocent.

For singles, it becomes more difficult to set these kinds of safeguards, but a single person could consider a site blocking program and allowing someone they trust to act as the administrator of the program. This would be a good idea especially if there have been problems with compromise on the computer in the past.

The main thing a discerning believer should do is to recognize the ever-increasing dangers of secular media influence and set boundaries for themselves.

LIMIT ACCESS AND USE

Have times when the cell phone is not on or available. Cell phones are a little different from landlines because they go everywhere you do and they also can do things a basic landline cannot, such as import texts and emails. These technologies increase the demand on our lives. People who might think twice about calling you think nothing about tying up your time with texting. Personally, I like having a landline or basic cell phone that is available only to a handful of people who can get in touch with me in the event of an emergency or serious issue. But, I also am afforded the feeling that I can turn off the "public" cell phone from time to time that always keeps me connected to something.

If you have a job that needs you to be on call, then consider getting a phone or beeper dedicated to that purpose only so you can have times your main phone is off and you can be separated from everyone who has your number.

Set days off from television, gaming, or from similar electronic toys. Use self-control and make a commitment to set your computer and Internet use aside and do other things. Time off reduces temptations, changes thinking, and also promotes other interests. It is like reminding the recovering alcoholic not to go to the bar! In a similar way, we have become addicts to the online world.

I am sure you have experienced something similar to me. We have sat in our living room while both my husband and myself are on our laptops, the television is running, and the kids are texting or talking on their phones! This is becoming the standard picture of an average modern-day family. Do you see my point? We're addicted to the digital age!

Too much of anything isn't healthy, and it isn't healthy for our discerning spirit to spend hours and days immersed in secular Internet and media activities without a defined break. There may not be anything wrong with a certain movie, but anything can become a problem when we watch it again and again. We put ourselves at risk by overfilling our minds with these things, even when they aren't outright wrong.

MAKE PERSONAL DECISIONS

This doesn't just apply to media involvement. Every discerning believer must make some solid personal decisions as to what activities are not appropriate for a Christian and then decide they won't engage in those things. That means they won't participate through digital involvement or other means. For example, a Christian should have the clear standard that adultery is sin and they will not commit adultery. To further that standard they also shouldn't watch adulterous situations on television or in movies. The same kind of Christian would also make the personal decisions to dress modestly and show poised social behaviors in a liberated and adulterous age.

This also means that a discerning Christian won't do something because everyone else is doing it. For example, I know countless Christians who are literally social networking junkies! Sure, a little social networking here and there may be harmless, but again, make personal decisions that set rules for you. A discerning believer will not base their involvement on what the rest of the world is doing. This kind of peer pressure is not limited to kids and teens. Adults fall into many forms of peer pressure as well.

For example, don't log in every night because all your closest friends or co-workers do. Don't give your kids online accounts based on all the demands from their social lives. Don't buy that new laptop just because you feel pressure from everyone at work. There is so much pressure from everywhere today to make us all feel that we *have* to buy this, have that, or sign up for something else. Make personal decisions that are right for you and your family.

REGULAR SPIRITUAL HOUSECLEANING

Take time on a regular basis to go through videos, games, reading material, music, television cable subscriptions, and similar items. Review everything and do what you might call a spiritual housecleaning. Look for items that at the time seemed innocent enough, but as you grew in your Christianity you decided were no longer appropriate for you. Perhaps your discernment wasn't up to par when you opted to get the item. Not all things to be reviewed have to be media based. Sometimes it's other kids' toys, clothing, home accessories, paintings, and more. Other times a spiritual housecleaning needs to occur on

Facebook, MySpace, or in your friendships in general. Perhaps there are subscriptions to memberships and catalogs that need to be cancelled.

Go through your house every so often and decide if there are any items that could be bringing the wrong influences and if they are weights and sin that need to be set aside. For most dedicated Christians, the culprit area is usually the items related to media, and a strong discerning believer will take time to review their collections once in a while.

Years ago our son, who was still quite young at the time, told us that he had a video game that scared him. The funny thing was it was a kid's game, and there wasn't anything seemingly violent about the game. It was a game from a popular kid's movie that came out way back when I was a child, so it wouldn't have been something we would normally be reserved about.

However, he just kept saying that something about the images on the game scared him. We finally took a second look and did notice that one of the character's faces had been drawn on the game cover with a rather ferocious expression. When we showed it to our son he said, "That's it! That's the face that scares me, and it also appears when you play the game!"

We don't always know what spiritual entities can be attached to some of these things. Agreeing with our son, we decided to destroy the game. Now again, I am not saying you have to go through your house like a fanatic throwing everything in the garbage, but you should do a regular spiritual housecleaning and get rid of things that may have the wrong influence attached to them.

Listen to your spirit and let the Holy Spirit guide you. When applicable, get the children involved. If you as a husband and wife don't initially agree that something should be thrown out, then my encouragement is to err on the safe side. I would rather get rid of it and do without something than have an item that is allowing the wrong influences or potentially evil spirits into my home. Numbers says:

> *Then ye shall drive out all the inhabitants of the land from before you, and destroy all their pictures, and destroy all their molten images, and quite pluck down all their high places* (Numbers 33:52).

Then after you clean things out, pray through your house and decree the angels' covering upon it.

DISCERNING HOW TO ESCAPE TEMPTATION

I am convinced that the increased temptations to sin and compromise today are heightened dramatically by the multimedia highway. I like to think of it the way the airports do security. Increased threat means increased security measures need to be added.

Discerning believers need to increase their security measures against temptation. Unfortunately, many are not taking the necessary steps to have the right measures in place and thus end up falling into the traps of the devil. To deal with the issues surrounding spiritual discernment, we simply have to talk about how to overcome the temptations of the devil, especially when they are coming more heavily in this digital age. The demon powers have gotten creative with their measures.

From divorce in the church at an all-time high—even affecting preachers at record levels—to the average church member who can't seem to quit viewing Internet pornography, we have to consider the effects the media generation is having on our lives. We also must look at how to counteract more effectively in our warfare.

In our years of pastoring, I always encounter people who are convinced that their particular situation exempts them from the ability to overcome. I hear countless people who will say, "But you simply don't understand." They will cite that it was their childhood that made their issue unique. There are always those who couldn't make their marriage work, but they were two supposedly-Christian people that just couldn't get along. Yet they feel they have a right to divorce because their situation was unique from anyone else. Others feel their sinful behaviors were justified because they were somehow mistreated.

Yet the need for every Christian to escape temptation is the same. Truthfully, none of us have any valid excuses for misbehavior. All of us are accountable and responsible as believers to uphold the commandments of Scripture in spite of our circumstances. We are expected to hold fast to what the Bible commands on love and forgiveness. We are expected to trust the biblical promises on divine healing, even when it looks like our situation turned out just the opposite. Each one of us has an obligation to holy living, even though we grew up in a dysfunctional childhood upbringing.

The real trouble for many is that the vehement temptations of the evil one are without relent in the day we are living. They are at the flood stage, and if many Christians don't start now to put their defense systems in place they will be overpowered.

Let's look at probably the most common verse in regards to overcoming temptation that is found in the Bible:

> *No temptation has seized you except what is common to man. And God is faithful; He will not let you be tempted beyond what you can bear. But when you are tempted, He will also provide a way out so that you can stand up under it* (1 Corinthians 10:13 NIV).

This common verse provides us the easiest simple formula for overcoming any form of temptation. If we learn God's formula, we can defeat the sore temptations of the day, even when they come from every angle on the multimedia highway!

1. *My temptation is not unique!* *"There hath no temptation taken you but such as is common to man"* (1 Cor. 10:13). First, this verse reminds me that there is not one single temptation the devil can offer on planet earth that is new and unique, exclusive to me. It means that whatever I am being tempted with today is not unique. I am not alone. Others have been through exactly what I have been through. Sure, some have failed, but others have come out on top in total victory. So that leaves me inexcusable. If others defeated the same demons of temptation, then so can I! This is the beginning of the equation in the Bible formula that defeats every temptation.

2. *God never leaves me during temptation.* *"God is faithful."* The problem with us is that during moments of temptation we leave God. He never leaves us, however. He is there to walk us through it if we will turn to Him. The problem begins when we feel more comfortable turning to our own ways, pleasures, and feelings during the tempting moment. When you are in a time of challenge, don't let feelings of condemnation cause you to run from God. Instead, that is the time you need to run to Him! Ask Him for help and call out to Him for answers. Tell Him how you feel and what you are dealing with. Let the power of the Holy Spirit be involved during a temptation. He doesn't mind!

3. *This temptation isn't as hard as it seems.* *"He will not let you be tempted beyond what you can bear."* This pretty much does away with the whole idea of "I couldn't help myself." It dispels all the grandiose excuses for why we couldn't overcome temptation or be obedient. I know this sounds completely unrealistic and impossible, but again, it's a walk of faith. Do we believe the Bible when it says we won't be tempted beyond what we can bear? This verse applies to every human in every imaginable situation! Whatever you are dealing with today—whatever bad habit, whatever binding

addiction—it isn't impossible for you to bear. That should let you know that God believes in your abilities. It is a revelation that you are greater than the temptation is. You are a more powerful warrior than the demons that drive you to that area of struggle. You aren't the underdog—you are the favored winner. One key step to overcoming the most ferocious temptations is to believe you are the stronger opponent.

4. ***Look for the escape!*** *"He will also provide a way out so that you can stand up under it."* The most encouraging part is that God always has an escape route. He always has a plan for you to rise above temptation. The Bible does give a few secrets that help. One escape route was when Jesus told His disciples that prayer will help you be an overcomer of temptation. He said, *"...Rise and pray, lest ye enter into temptation"* (Luke 22:46). In other words, if you will pray when temptation comes, you won't enter into it.

Now it isn't too deep and revelatory, but the Bible also has another route of escape. *"Thy word have I hid in mine heart, that I might not sin against Thee"* (Ps. 119:11). The more of God's Word we put in our heart, the more we are empowered to defeat temptation.

Lastly, never forget that God always has a unique plan of escape for you, assuming you have been first utilizing the power of prayer and the Word. Armed with these two primary weapons, God has a tailor-made plan for your situation. The problem many of us have is we don't look for any escape routes. We only look at the prison. For some, the escape route God has might be as simple as adjusting a few things in your schedule. For others, it could be admitting the need for repentance. If you will ask the Holy Spirit, He will guide you into the truth. The key is to look for the escape.

As we are further immersed in this media-crazed generation, we need to heighten our discernment, fight the subtle devices of temptation, and double-check our doctrine and beliefs. This media onslaught will make the challenge to stay on the path of God more difficult, and the demonic deceptions are more subtle than ever. We will see along the way many who will change or forget their doctrinal beliefs; some will give in to depravity, and others will take on a view of Christianity that befriends worldly thinking. We are in an hour that requires a new level of warfare, spiritual alertness, and endurance in order to defeat temptation.

> *Take heed unto thyself, and unto the doctrine; continue in them: for in doing this thou shalt both save thyself, and them that hear thee* (1 Timothy 4:16).

There's an old saying: "It's no longer business as usual." We can no longer take a casual approach to defeating temptation. The war for our very salvation is deceptively subtle, but stronger than it has ever been. Make a strong commitment to discern when temptation is lurking at your doorstep. Never forget that, though it may involve some spiritual and personal warfare, there is an eternal blessing behind it.

> *Blessed is the man that endureth temptation: for when he is tried, he shall receive the crown of life, which the Lord hath promised to them that love Him* (James 1:12).

In this hour, we must discern ourselves, our beliefs, and our actions. By doing so, we truly will save ourselves from the raging temptations increased by living in this media generation.

Chapter Ten

WHO IS ON THE LORD'S SIDE?

Then shall ye return, and discern between
the righteous and the wicked, between
him that serveth God and him that
serveth Him not (Malachi 3:18).

They were so well-known, so respected by everyone. More than likely, they enjoyed the recognition they had among all the people. Because of their fame, it wasn't hard for them to gather a crowd. Fame does something to people. Not only does it affect the famous, but it affects the people who consider them famous. When used wrongly, the famous can use their position to take advantage of people and draw them to themselves for selfish reasons. In turn, those who love the influential and famous will often believe and follow them into almost any idea.

On this occasion, a group of influential people gathered some of the most respected leaders in Israel. Perhaps you know them? Their names were Korah, Dathan, and Abiram, and their story is found in Numbers 16. These men used their position of fame to draw people away from God and Moses and toward themselves. Numbers 16:1-3 says Korah *"took men"* who were *"two hundred and fifty princes of the assembly, famous in the congregation, men of renown: and they gathered themselves together against Moses...."*

The matter of Korah is probably one of the best examples in Scripture that helps us determine how to discern who is on the Lord's side and who is not. That is because in this story, Moses and the children of Israel were dealing with a unique situation. This time they weren't fighting the Egyptians, the Amalekites, or the Canaanites. These men were a part of their assembly, part of the people of the Lord who had earned respect and position within the camp of Israel. They were trusted by the people.

Now this is where deciding who is really for God becomes the most difficult, and believers have the hardest time discerning where to stand. That is because they aren't dealing with the Hollywood actor or the politician who defies the Gospel. They are dealing with friends— people they have grown to love and appreciate. They are dealing with preachers whom they have respected over the years and who can bring people to their feet during their sermons. They are dealing with fellow church members and co-laborers in the faith. This is where discerning who is for the Lord and who is not is becoming a mighty challenge. This was the case with Korah. The compromisers were from within their own camp, and the people had a hard time believing it.

Jesus said this would be a factor in our commitment to proclaim the Gospel of the Kingdom. That sometimes it would separate you from people you love, making it all the more challenging. Look at what He said:

> *Think not that I am come to send peace on earth: I came not to send peace, but a sword. For I am come to set a man at variance against his father, and the daughter against her mother, and the daughter in law against her mother in law. And a man's foes shall be they of his own household* (Matthew 10:34-36).

Of course, Jesus could certainly be referring to the unsaved and saved persons who live in the same family. However, we also have to look at the real fact that Jesus also showed that the Gospel would divide the truly spiritual believers from the carnal ones who refuse to give up certain behaviors. The Word of God in unadulterated form will automatically separate the flesh from the spirit (see Heb. 4:12). We talked earlier in Mark 3:33-35 about how Jesus said that the true members of His family were those who do the will of God, not so much natural blood relatives or even friends and acquaintances. In His mind, the ones He was going to remain connected to were those who were committed to pursuing a life of righteousness.

Many church people and Christians have a hard time with this part of discernment. They like the Kingdom until it requires them to discern the truth and perhaps change the dynamics of certain relationships or even perhaps give up some altogether. They often argue and find reasons why certain friends and relationships aren't harmful because after all, "We go to the same church," or "We have known them for years."

It was clear in Numbers 16 that God had to separate the righteous from the unrighteous right from within the camp of Israel. He separated the rebellious and fleshly from those who were obedient and dedicated to Him. If you look again at the story, you find that

Korah made the same key argument against Moses that we see in the modern-day church. Korah said:

> *They came as a group to oppose Moses and Aaron and said to them, "You have gone too far! The whole community is holy, every one of them, and the Lord is with them. Why then do you set yourselves above the Lord's assembly?"* (Numbers 16:3 NIV)

Notice what Korah's group brought up. They said, *"The whole community is holy, **every one** of them."* They wanted to prove that Moses was at fault, while every person in the congregation was unquestionably considered holy. They didn't want to admit the possibility that there might be carnal compromisers within the ranks.

This is a common problem today. People automatically assume that all their friends in the church are holy and spiritual. They are often quicker to blame the pastor of wrongdoing than their fellow pew members. People think just because their friends or relatives go to a good church and speak in tongues that these people are right with God.

I believe this long-time tendency is nearly at epidemic proportions in churches today because people are less quick to separate righteousness from unrighteousness. A false concept of love and grace gives the underlying idea that everyone is wonderful in the church, almost to the point that any discernment or correction of sin is considered overbearing.

Korah's intent was to make it look like everyone in the congregation was righteous, so God had to bring a defining moment to prove otherwise. There needed to be a set time of separation among the people so it would become obvious who truly was righteous and willing to stand on the Lord's side.

Let's look briefly at what happened when Moses confronts Korah.

Then he said to Korah and all his followers: "In the morning the Lord will show who belongs to Him and who is holy, and He will have that person come near Him. The man He chooses He will cause to come near Him" (Numbers 16:5 NIV).

God was preparing the camp for a moment of divine separation. Based on the events leading up to this, the camp of Israel had been struggling to stay with the Lord. They were constantly distracted by carnal, lustful behaviors to the point that the Lord's anger was kindled against them more than once. Then, when the people demanded flesh to eat, God was angry and sent a plague (see Num. 11:4,33-34). The Bible says that the problem with Israel was they were constantly being persuaded by a mixed multitude of foreigners that followed them out of Egypt. *"And the mixt multitude that was among them fell a lusting..."* (Num. 11:4). This mixed multitude came along to benefit themselves. They were looking for what was in it for them.

This is the same kind of "mixed multitude" we see in churches. There are always those who aren't in it because of their dedicated love to Jesus alone. Some come to God because they hit rock bottom and need a brief pick-me-up. I have seen many of these people serve God for a season, even several years, but when the test is upon them and a tempting persuasion arises, they go back to "Egypt;" they go back to the world. Some of the mixed multitude in our churches are those who want a God who gives them peace but requires very little lifestyle change. These people believe they were pretty good when they came into Christianity, and so now the dimension of Christianity is only to enhance what they have already created. They don't expect any heavy price tags to be attached to it. Others are long-time, even Spirit-filled believers who never completely crucify themselves from some of the carnality of this world. Some of these have even entered a dimension of spiritual blindness and pride because they won't address their habits and issues.

Many in these groups won't stay so "Christian" when the challenges are upon them, and they always end up influencing the people of God with the wrong things.

God needed to remove the mixed multitude from Israel because they were pulling the true people of God down and drawing them away from what was right. Moses tells Korah to gather censers, which were fire pans used for burning incense. Incense in the Old Testament always represented holiness and obedience to God. God had a specific type of incense which He commanded the sons of Levi to burn in the holy place. When God's pure incense was burned, it gave off a smoke with a sweet scent. Any other counterfeit incense spoke of a lack of holiness and obedience. It spoke of sin and rebellion against God's ways. When burned, it would result in a foreign smell, and the fire of God would then destroy the ones who burned it (see Exod. 30:9).

The sons of Aaron once tried to offer foreign incense before the Lord. The Bible says they offered *"strange fire"* (see Lev. 10:1; Num. 26:61). When God smelled the wrong odor, His fire then destroyed them.

Notice that it took fire to reveal the ingredients of the incense. In our lives, it takes fire to reveal what kind of "incense" we are carrying around. You can always tell what is in people when they are put into the fiery furnace of testing. When they are under temptation by the devil, their level of holiness is revealed by how they respond. When they are in a time of financial challenge, their true level of faith is revealed beyond how they worship and act in church on Sunday. Suddenly, the kind of "incense" they are offering up is proven. If they have compromise or wrong motives, their actions give off a foul odor. The day of adversity or fire will tell a lot about you (see Prov. 24:10). God and everyone around you will see if you are offering up "strange fire."

Moses had Korah and his 250 men bring their censers of incense and put fire under them. Of course, as we see through the chapter, they hadn't even lit the fires before their true colors were coming out.

They were already accusing Moses of abusing his leadership simply because he stood up in his God-given position, commanding righteousness. Dathan and Abiram initially refused to offer their incense. They were probably afraid because they knew what sinful things existed in the deep cupboards of their lives! So in Numbers 16:12-14, they shifted the attention off themselves and onto Moses, accusing him of taking advantage of them.

We see this in churches too these days. People don't want their unholy incense to be seen, so they shift the blame onto the pastor or others in order to cover for themselves. A lot of times their accusations are not much different from Dathan and Abiram, who said:

> *Isn't it enough that you have brought us up out of a land flowing with milk and honey to kill us in the desert? And now you also want to lord it over us? Moreover, you haven't brought us into a land flowing with milk and honey or given us an inheritance of fields and vineyards. Will you gouge out the eyes of these men? No, we will not come!* (Numbers 16:13-14 NIV)

They accused Moses of mistreating them and promising things they didn't feel were coming to pass in their estimation. They also accused Moses of being too controlling. I believe it was to cover for the real reason they didn't want to show up and offer their fire. They didn't want their true "incense" to be revealed.

Nonetheless, Moses got Korah to gather everyone the next day. Apparently Korah had the biggest influence, because all 250 of his followers showed up. They lit their censers of incense at the door of the tabernacle, and suddenly the glory of the Lord appeared.

Immediately, God smelled their strange fire and said, *"Separate yourselves from among this congregation, that I may consume them in a moment"* (Num. 16:21). This was going to be the defining moment revealing who was really with the Lord. Knowing that God was going to destroy those who offered strange fire, Moses warned the people to get away from the tents of Korah, Dathan, and Abiram. Moses was about to prove to the congregation, by the catastrophic way Korah and these men were going to die, that God was upon Him. He said:

> But if the Lord brings about something totally new,
> and the earth opens its mouth and swallows them,
> with everything that belongs to them, and they go
> down alive into the grave, then you will know that
> these men have treated the Lord with contempt
> (Numbers 16:30 NIV).

Of course it happened. Korah, Dathan, and Abiram and their children died as the earth opened up and swallowed them along with all their belongings. The Bible says you could hear their screams. Then the fire of the Lord followed up and consumed the remaining 250 famous men of influence. That is why it is so important to discern who you decide to follow, whether it be preachers or just friends and church people that have influential personalities.

Afterwards, Aaron the priest was instructed to take their censers that burned strange fire and beat them into plates that were to be placed on the altar as a hallowed sign to the children of Israel. The sign was this: *"That no stranger...come near to offer incense before the Lord"* (Num. 16:40). There was to be no unholy scent coming into the presence of the Lord.

Of course, you would think that would have been all the congregation needed to remind them that they cannot keep company with those of the world or mixed multitude, but it wasn't. Instead they began to accuse Moses and said, *"...Ye have killed the people of the Lord"* (Num. 16:41).

This is also a common problem in churches. Instead of Christians separating themselves from carnal people like this, they defend them. Some have committed adultery, swindled people out of money, or lied and cheated right in the church. When you hold them accountable, they will get angry and leave. I have watched some of those same people after they leave the church go back to sin or secular living. Often, you see these people walk out the consequences of wrong choices months or years later.

Yet even with all of that, you will still have people who will tell the pastor he was too harsh. When the pastor deals with them and says this behavior won't be tolerated and that they need to come clean and repent, some people will say the pastor was mean to them. It sounds just like the story of Israel and Korah who accused Moses of killing the "holy" people of the Lord. Remember how Korah said, "Every one of them is holy." That's the big deception—everyone just thinks everyone is holy when they aren't.

So God had to bring yet another separation. God's anger began to consume the people with a plague and 14,700 people died that day.

We see these "seasons" of separation that God periodically brought among the children of Israel because of the mixed multitude among them. One of the most unforgettable examples is when they worshiped the golden calf and Moses commanded, saying, *"Who is on the Lord's side? Let him come unto me"* (Exod. 32:26). Those who didn't were plagued. God had to define who was committed to live right and who wasn't, and He did so in such a way that it was obvious to the entire congregation.

SEASONS OF SEPARATION

I believe that just as the children of Israel had to walk through these seasons of separation, the Lord is separating the righteous from the unrighteous in the Church. Of course, He doesn't plague people under the grace of the New Covenant the way it was under the old. However, we can be disciplined by God (see Heb. 12:6-9). The Bible also says that we not only reap what we sow, but if we refuse God's voice of correction we risk suffering the results when the heavens and earth are shaken (see Gal. 6:7; Heb. 12:25-29). Essentially, rebellious disobedience subjects us to the same consequences and judgments of those in the world.

God is bringing a time of divine separation of the wheat and tares so we will know in these last days who is truly on the Lord's side.

It is becoming increasingly hard to discern the difference, but the heat is being turned up and things are going to start coming to light. The world in this last age is becoming a more unstable place, full of trials and increased trouble all around. It's going to bring the dross to the surface as the Church is tried by the fires of life in this world. The scent of our incense is going to become clear. Those who refuse to let go of their carnality and secret sin and even those who hide behind religious gimmicks will begin to stand out when the fire burns hotter. These won't be able to stand the heat, so they will give in to whatever enticing deceptions promise to rescue them from their problems. They also won't look highly on the ones who refuse to give in or unite with their carnality. Chances are, we will see a group like the men of Korah who accused the true people of God of overstepping their bounds and of being inconsiderate and too extreme. Like Jesus said, *"And a man's foes shall be they of his own household"* (Matt. 10:36).

Yet those who are willing to return to the Lord and walk through the fire in holiness will come out as pure gold and give off the scent of pure incense. They will be able to discern who and what is truly on the Lord's side.

For some, it will mean they won't be able to hang out with certain friends at church anymore because of their behaviors and lifestyle. Perhaps they were once best friends and even ministered together in the prayer team, but somewhere their friend developed a divisive spirit or area of compromise. Those who want to live holy realize that they can't hang around the mixed multitude. They can't buy their books, listen to their sermons, or just hang with them after church.

I believe that in preparation for the Lord's return prophetically the Church is entering seasons of separation. First, we are entering Second Corinthians 6:17, which says, *"Wherefore come out from among them, and be ye separate, saith the Lord, and touch not the unclean thing; and I will receive you."* We are going to have to be willing to separate ourselves from darkness, even when it hits close to home. That is really where the mixed multitude lives—right in our own camps, homes, and churches. It's one thing if our moral ideals are challenged through a television program, even though that deceives enough Christians by itself. But when it's a family member, friend, or preacher we love, it becomes harder. Confusing emotions and relationship issues get in the way as you hear people you are close to say things that make you wonder if your version of Christianity is too extreme. Suddenly, you are made to feel like an outsider among those you love or have come to appreciate in some way. The Church is at a place where it must be separate from the mixed multitude that dwells among them.

Second, once we *are* willing to stand out and be separate at all costs, the Lord is going to give us the ability to discern between the righteous and the unrighteous, even when personal circumstances muddy the waters. The church is also entering Malachi 3:18, which says:

> *Then shall ye return, and discern between the righteous and the wicked, between him that serveth God and him that serveth Him not.*

As I look through the Scriptures, I believe there are five key areas or levels of separation we will have to encounter. Just as the children of Israel experienced several of these separations from the mixed multitude, so must the holy remnant church be separated.

SEPARATION FROM WORLDLINESS

Ye adulterers and adulteresses, know ye not that the friendship of the world is enmity with God? whosoever therefore will be a friend of the world is the enemy of God (James 4:4).

Godliness and worldliness just don't mix. The reason this verse of Scripture uses the phase *"adulterers and adulteresses"* is not to be crass. It is because this is how God see worldliness. He sees it as a disloyalty of our heart commitment to Him. God doesn't want us to fit in with a worldly system that He is eventually going to judge and do away with. This world's systems and principles will one day be destroyed. We can't let them adulterate our thinking just because they sound educated and reasonable.

If we hang out with worldly friends, eventually we will begin to think like them, dress like them, act like them, and talk their language. Many of these worldly behaving folks sit in our Spirit-filled churches. So many Christians these days are doing their level best to get as close to the edge as they can. They dress in such a way so as not to be totally immodest, but they push the envelope by lowering their blouse line and shortening their skirts just a tad bit more. Now we have people getting "Christian" tattoos; even preachers are starting to sport them as a new fad. We need to be separate from the world's methods, appearances, and lifestyles.

Some people are sorely fooling themselves into thinking they can hang on the edge of worldly living and still be a Christian. That is a deceptive lie and it is impossible to do. Worldliness causes God to view you as His enemy.

SEPARATION FROM THE WORLD'S APPLAUSE

"Woe unto you, when all men shall speak well of you! for so did their fathers to the false prophets" (Luke 6:26). As I already mentioned, many believers want to present the world with a version of Christianity that makes them feel we are all on the same page. It's like we don't want them to think we are too away from them and that Christianity can easily fit in with their current lifestyles. I think the church is coming to a crossroad where we will have to decide whether we will invite men's applause or be willing to accept their disdain. It seems many are leaning toward gaining their applause because we think that is our path to "winning" them over. Actually, it seems that instead of winning them we are misleading them. We are allowing them to believe they don't have to change much to be a Christian, when that is the farthest thing from the truth.

Of course, I am not saying this means we need to purposely try to anger everyone. We just need to preach the sacrificial Kingdom the way Jesus and the early church did and let the chips fall where they may. We need to present a pure Gospel that will undoubtedly offend some who hear it, but that will also draw many to Jesus Christ.

SEPARATION FROM THE WICKEDNESS
OF THE PRESENT GENERATION

"And with many other words did he testify and exhort, saying, Save yourselves from this untoward generation" (Acts 2:40). This verse was a part of Peter's sermon delivered on the Day of Pentecost. There was a reason he addressed the generation in particular. I believe this was because there are certain evil patterns and trends that are specific to each generation. Peter was warning them to be aware of the sins and traps that were most predominant to the time in which they were living. Part of our separation means that we have to recognize the

evils that are specific to our day. There are certain deceptions and sins that affect generations differently. In fact, similar to angels, demons have assignments, some of which are released at specific times and seasons. We can see that there were certain evils present in the early church, and while those evils are still present today they appear in different packages and affect the people differently.

For example, we talked about the digital age which is one of the methods the devil is capitalizing upon in this present generation. Another package the devil is utilizing is sports and fitness. Just like digital technology, sports and fitness has its place, but we also can't be drawn in by a generation that has fallen into sports and fitness idolatry. Even the health and wellness movement we see today can get over into extremes where people are bound to herbs and potions, worship of the body, and even vanity.

We need to separate ourselves from the potential deceptions that are affecting this generation.

SEPARATION BY REPROVING DARKNESS

"And have no fellowship with the unfruitful works of darkness, but rather reprove them" (Eph. 5:11). One key level of separation is that we are called to speak out against the works of darkness. We are called to speak up about sin. We need to stand against the issues that want to be set up opposite of the Bible. We have to be willing to speak up when called upon and sometimes when not called upon. Our voice of righteousness needs to be heard in our work places, our churches, in politics, courtrooms, and in the media. We cannot remain silent with the truth. Sure we need to be tasteful and statesmanlike, but we also need to be like John the Baptist, a voice crying and saying, *"...Prepare ye the way of the Lord..."* (Matt. 3:3).

Pastors need to preach honestly and boldly. They can't shy away from certain verses of Scripture that might make people nervous. We need to preach honestly about eternity. We need to demonstrate the Holy Spirit and power.

Christian parents need to hold their children accountable to a righteous standard and not think it harmless to fit in with secular friends and compromising choices in entertainment.

When we see wrong, especially that which comes in contact with our own sphere of influence, we need to speak up and make our voice of righteousness heard.

SEPARATION FROM CARNAL CHRISTIANS

Now we command you, brethren, in the name of our Lord Jesus Christ, that ye withdraw yourselves from every brother that walketh disorderly, and not after the tradition which he received of us (2 Thessalonians 3:6).

This wasn't a suggestion by the apostle Paul; it was a direct command. Strong Christians need to separate themselves from carnal believers. These are those who don't want to change certain lifestyle patterns or attitudes. They often have some sin habits they refuse to deal with. Some are simply those who aren't committed to church and only attend sporadically. The overall fruit of their lives is up and down and they can't ever show strides toward spiritual maturity.

Be discerning on who your close friends are. This is not the hour to be hanging around with compromisers in Christendom. We need to withdraw from these people. If they don't encourage us to be stronger in the Lord but rather draw us down, then it's time to find new friends. If not, their disorderly behavior *will* eventually rub off on us. You may not think they have the power to affect you in a negative way, but they will. You become like what you hang around. Be careful not to be found defending and befriending the mixed multitude.

These five levels of separation will be present in the last-days church as God divides those who are of Him. There will be a price to pay sometimes to walk on that path, but if we take that road it will eventually lead to a crown of life.

NARROW IS THE WAY

As we have covered the many things we need to discern in our modern day throughout this book and the skills needed for excellent discernment, we need to talk briefly about the road that leads to life.

Lately, many people are adapting the idea that there are many ways to God. While Christian groups aren't blatantly saying that there are other ways besides Jesus, they *are* giving direct and indirect impressions that when people *do* come to Christ they can define what level of Christianity works for them. In other words, if your way of coming is by going to church once a month then that is acceptable for you. Or if your way of coming to Christ is by praying a prayer but then being allowed to choose what level of depth you want beyond that, then this is OK because after all, "It's what you can do." We allow people to serve God on their terms.

We cannot define for ourselves today what Christianity means. We cannot define what the road to life looks like according to our own definitions. We need to define it according to the Bible.

Jesus defined it plainly. He said it is narrow (see Matt. 7:14). That means you cannot veer too far or you will be off the right road. As we conclude our discussion on discernment we need to end by making sure we do two key things in our lives.

1. *Stay on the narrow road to life.*

We will have to live restricted to the narrow path. Many people are against the phrase "narrow minded." And of course, I am not advocating strange religious fanaticism such as telling women they need to wear a pilgrim dress in order to be modest. I am saying we need to be narrow minded when it comes to borderline sins, compromises, worldly ideals, and new lifestyles that promise liberty when in fact all they are doing is putting us on the wide road to destruction. Keep yourself in check in these last days. Repent quickly when you have sinned, and set boundaries for yourself that are in line with the Word of God.

2. *Let the truth set you free.*

Jesus said the truth isn't a form of bondage as some might want us to believe. Some think that living in the truth is to going to snuff out all your fun and happiness. Instead, when we "imprison" ourselves to the truth, that is the only time the shackles of bondage come off and we are made free (see John 8:32). Face the truth in this hour. Sometimes it isn't what we want to hear, and sometimes it will make us uncomfortable. Truth can mess with your emotions and cause you to have to make some hard decisions about your life.

In these last days, hold yourself accountable to the Word of God above all else! Let it be your standard for everything you do, say, and believe in. Double check yourself and your doctrinal beliefs against it on an ongoing basis. If you will imprison yourself to the truth, you will surely be made free!

As we enter the final hours of the last days, we will come out in victory if we have the right skills for discernment in place. A discerning Christian is a strong Christian, because they will walk in truth, they will run from sin, and they will oppose evil. Let's be part of the remnant church so needed today that will stand out as experts who are well equipped with the ability to discern the spirit of error and thereby decode hell's deceptive propaganda!

Other Books by Brenda Kunneman

When Your Life Has Been Tampered With

The Supernatural You

ONE VOICE MINISTRIES
THE MINISTRY OF HANK & BRENDA KUNNEMAN

CONFERENCES

Hank and Brenda travel globally ministering in churches, conferences and conventions. They bring relevant biblical messages from a prophetic viewpoint, and their dynamic preaching style is coupled with the demonstrations of the Holy Spirit. Though they preach at events separately, they are especially known for their unique platform of ministry together as a team in the ministry of the gifts of the Spirit. For additional information about scheduling a ministry or church conference with Hank and/or Brenda you may contact One Voice Ministries at 402.896.6692 or you may request a ministry packet online at ovm.org

BOOKS, PRODUCTS AND RESOURCES

Books, audio and video material are available at the Kunneman's online store at ovm.org. Book titles include, *When Your Life Has Been Tampered With, Don't Leave God Alone, The Supernatural You, The Revealer of Secrets,* and *Hide and Seek, & Chaos in the King's Court.* The One Voice Ministries' Website also provides many ministry resources including Hank's page called *Prophetic Perspectives,* providing excerpts and prophetic insight on world events. Brenda's page, *The Daily Prophecy,* is a daily prophetic word which has changed lives around the world. There are also numerous articles for study.

LORD OF HOSTS CHURCH

Hank and Brenda Kunneman also pastor Lord of Hosts Church in Omaha, Nebraska. Combined with sound teaching, captivating praise and worship and a prophetic flair, services at Lord of Hosts Church are always rich with the presence of God. Lord of Hosts Church is known for its solid team of leaders, organized style and ministry that touches the everyday needs of people. Through the many avenues of ministry the church is raising up strong believers. Many ministries globally have referred to Lord of Hosts Church to be among the most up and coming, cutting-edge churches in the United States. Further information about Lord of Hosts Church can be found by calling 402.896.6692 or online at lohchurch.org and ovm.org

PASTORS HANK AND BRENDA KUNNEMAN
LORD OF HOSTS CHURCH & ONE VOICE MINISTRIES
5351 S. 139th Plaza • Omaha, Nebraska 68137
Phone: (402) 896-6692 • Fax: (402) 894-9068
ovm.org • lohchurch.org

In the right hands, This Book will Change Lives!

Most of the people who need this message will not be looking for this book. To change their lives, you need to put a copy of this book in their hands.

> *But others (seeds) fell into good ground, and brought forth fruit, some a hundred-fold, some sixty-fold, some thirty-fold* (Matthew 13:8).

Our ministry is constantly seeking methods to find the good ground, the people who need this anointed message to change their lives. Will you help us reach these people?

> *Remember this—a farmer who plants only a few seeds will get a small crop. But the one who plants generously will get a generous crop* (2 Corinthians 9:6).

EXTEND THIS MINISTRY BY SOWING
3 BOOKS, 5 BOOKS, 10 BOOKS, **OR MORE TODAY,**
AND BECOME A LIFE CHANGER!

Thank you,

Don Nori Sr., Publisher
Destiny Image
Since 1982

DESTINY IMAGE PUBLISHERS, INC.

*"Speaking to the Purposes of God for This Generation
and for the Generations to Come."*

VISIT OUR NEW SITE HOME AT
WWW.DESTINYIMAGE.COM

FREE SUBSCRIPTION TO DI NEWSLETTER

Receive free unpublished articles by top DI authors, exclusive

discounts, and free downloads from our best and newest books.

Visit www.destinyimage.com to subscribe.

Write to: Destiny Image
             P.O. Box 310
             Shippensburg, PA 17257-0310

Call: 1-800-722-6774

Email: orders@destinyimage.com

For a complete list of our titles or to place an order
online, visit www.destinyimage.com.

FIND US ON FACEBOOK OR FOLLOW US ON TWITTER.

www.facebook.com/destinyimage   **facebook**
www.twitter.com/destinyimage   **twitter**

41101256R00144